ENJOYING KINGDOM PROSPERITY

God's Purpose for Prosperity in The Life of A Believer

David S. Philemon

Royal Diadem Publishing Inc.

Dedication

To the Almighty God, my Rock, Refuge, and Source of all wisdom and strength. Thank You for Your unwavering love, grace, and the purpose You've placed within me. May this book bring glory to Your name and draw others closer to You.

And to my beloved spiritual parents, Dr. Paul and Dr. Mrs. Becky Paul Enenche, who have faithfully nurtured and guided me in this journey. Your example of unwavering devotion, godly counsel, and compassionate care has been a beacon of light and strength in my life. Thank you for standing as pillars of faith and for your steadfast commitment to the Kingdom.

ACKNOWLEDGMENT

This book would not have been possible without the unwavering support, dedication, and talent of an extraordinary team. My deepest gratitude goes to each of you for your contributions, insights, and encouragement throughout this journey.

First and foremost, thank you to Rev. Mimi Philemon my dear wife, Rev. Shina Gentry, and and my assistant pastor Rev. Bright Amudoaghan for your incredible effort, encouragement, and belief in this project. Your support has been instrumental in bringing this vision to life.

To the dedicated leaders of Royal Diadem Publishing, Ide Imogie and Kishawna Bailey, I am immensely grateful for your belief in this project from the very beginning and for investing your time and energy into its development. Your creativity, dedication, and expertise have been the backbone of this endeavor.

I am especially grateful to the Royal Diadem Publishing team— Beulah Orogun, Emmanuella Ben-Eboh, Doyinsade Awodele, Kim Matthews, and Shante Gill, for your meticulous attention to detail, refining every page and ensuring that each word reflects our vision.

A heartfelt thank you to my family, friends, and colleagues whose unwavering support and belief in this project gave me the courage and strength to see it through.

Finally, thank you to all the readers and supporters who make this work meaningful. I am humbled and honored to share this journey with each of you.

With all my gratitude,
David Philemon

CONTENTS

INTRODUCTION

Understanding God's Plan For Wealth

Wealth and prosperity are subjects that often stir mixed emotions among Christians. Many believers struggle to reconcile the idea of pursuing financial success with the teachings of Jesus, who spoke of humility, helping the poor, and storing up treasures in heaven rather than seeking material riches. This tension leads to confusion. Can a Christian be wealthy? Is it wrong to pursue financial success? The answer in Scripture is clear: wealth, when viewed through God's Word, has a greater purpose than personal gain. It can be a powerful tool for advancing God's Kingdom and fulfilling His plan on Earth. The Bible is filled with examples of godly individuals blessed with wealth.

People like Abraham (Genesis 13:2), Job (Job 1:3), and Solomon (1 Kings 10:23) were richly blessed by God, not just for their own sake, but for a greater purpose. Their wealth allowed them to influence others, extend generosity, and fulfill God's plans. At the same time, Scripture clarifies that wealth is not the ultimate goal. In Matthew 6:19-21, Jesus teaches: "Lay not up for yourselves treasures upon earth, where moth and rust doth corrupt, and where thieves break through and steal: But lay up for yourselves treasures in heaven... For where your treasure is, there will your heart be also." Christians should focus not on earthly riches alone but on aligning their hearts with God's eternal purposes. It's important to understand that wealth is a blessing from God, but it comes with responsibilities. Deuteronomy 8:18 reminds us: "But thou shalt remember the LORD thy God: for it is he that giveth thee power to get wealth, that he may establish his covenant which he swore unto thy fathers, as it is this day." God gives the ability to gain wealth, not just for personal comfort, but to further His work on earth. Therefore, Christians are called to manage their wealth with a mindset focused on God's Kingdom.

Wealth, in the eyes of God, is not merely for our benefit but serves a larger purpose in advancing His Kingdom. Financial resources can enable the gospel's spread, provide for those in need, and support ministries that share God's love with the world. 1 Timothy 6:17-18 guides those blessed with wealth: "Charge them that are rich in this world, that they are not high-minded, nor trust in uncertain riches, but in the living God... They do good, are rich in good works, ready to distribute, willing to communicate." This shows that wealth is not condemned; it must be used wisely —rich in good works, ready to give, and eager to share with others. When believers recognize that their financial blessings are tools for kingdom impact, they gain a new perspective on wealth. Instead of seeking wealth for personal satisfaction, they use it to further God's work. Whether through giving to the church, supporting missionaries, or helping the poor, wealth becomes a powerful resource for a believer with the right heart.

One of the most essential principles of wealth is stewardship. Stewardship means managing what God has given us in a way that pleases Him. Everything we have—our money, time, talents, and resources—comes from God. Psalm 24:1 says: "The earth is the LORD's, and the fulness thereof; the world, and they that dwell therein." Since God owns all things, we are simply caretakers of what He has entrusted us. Jesus' parable of the talents in Matthew 25:14-30 illustrates this well. In the story, a master gave talents (a form of money to three of his servants. Two invested their abilities and earned more, but one buried his talent out of fear and did nothing with it. When the master returned, he praised the two servants who had been faithful to what they were given and rebuked the one who had wasted his opportunity. This teaches us that God expects us to use our resources wisely. We are accountable for managing His blessings, whether we have much or little. Stewardship involves using wealth not just for personal needs but for the glory of God. It's about wisely planning, saving, and investing, all while seeking God's guidance to use our resources for His Kingdom's best.

Another critical aspect of God's plan for wealth is generosity. Throughout Scripture, God calls His people to be generous with their resources. Proverbs 11:25 says: "The liberal soul shall be made fat: and he that watereth shall be watered also himself." This means that when we give generously, we, too, are blessed in return. God loves a cheerful giver, as 2 Corinthians 9:7 says: "Every man according as he purposeth in his heart, so let him give; not grudgingly, or of necessity: for God loveth a cheerful giver." Generosity reflects the heart of God, who gave His only Son for us (John 3:16. As followers of Christ, we are called to mirror this giving spirit. Whether through financial gifts, time, or service, our generosity is a way to show God's love to others. Giving also teaches us to trust in God rather than our wealth. When we give, we acknowledge that everything we have comes from Him and that He is our ultimate provider. For some believers, God's plan for wealth includes the path of entrepreneurship and business. Running a business or engaging in entrepreneurship can be more than just a way to earn money—it can be a divine calling that allows believers to serve others, solve problems, and create jobs. Through entrepreneurship, believers can live out biblical principles like integrity, hard work, and stewardship, all while bringing light to the marketplace. In the Bible, successful businesspeople used their resources to further God's Kingdom. Lydia, a seller of purple cloth, was a successful businesswoman who supported Paul's ministry and helped the early church (Acts 16:14-15. Through her business, Lydia had the means to contribute to God's work. Entrepreneurship is a unique way to bring God's influence into the business world. Colossians 3:23 reminds us: "And whatsoever ye do, do it heartily, as to the Lord, and not unto men." Whether working in business or ministry, believers are called to do everything for the glory of God. By following biblical principles in business, entrepreneurs can create an atmosphere where Christ-like values are evident and financial success is tied to God's mission.

While wealth can be a blessing, it also brings challenges. There is a temptation to trust in riches instead of trusting in God. Proverbs 11:28 warns: "He that trusteth in his riches shall fall: but the righteous shall flourish as a branch." Jesus also warned against serving wealth: "Ye cannot serve God and mammon" (Matthew 6:24. Believers must guard their hearts against the love of money and the dangers of pride. Instead, they are called to trust God, knowing He is the provider. 1 Timothy 6:10 cautions: "For the love of money is the root of all evil." Wealth itself is not evil, but the love of it can lead to many harmful choices. Finally, part of God's plan for wealth involves leaving a legacy. Proverbs 13:22 says: "A good man leaveth an inheritance to his children's children." Wealth is not just for us to enjoy during our lifetime; it is something we can pass on to bless future generations. This includes not only financial wealth but also a spiritual legacy. Believers are called to teach their children the principles of stewardship, generosity, and faithfulness to God, ensuring their legacy impacts future generations for God's Kingdom. God's plan for wealth is much more than accumulating material things. It's about using financial resources for a higher purpose—building His Kingdom, helping others, and leaving a legacy that honors Him. Matthew 6:33 perfectly summarizes this truth: "But seek ye first the kingdom of God, and his righteousness; and all these things shall be added unto you." When believers prioritize God's Kingdom, wealth becomes a tool for His glory, and prosperity follows as part of His plan for our lives.

CHAPTER 1

BIBLICAL FOUNDATIONS OF WEALTH AND PROSPERITY

T he Bible speaks a lot about wealth, prosperity, and material blessings. However, these ideas are often misunderstood or seen as conflicting with Christian values. Many believers struggle to reconcile pursuing financial success with their faith, thinking it is wrong to desire wealth. But the Bible teaches that wealth is a blessing from God when used correctly. This chapter will explore the biblical foundation for wealth and prosperity, showing how God's plan for His people includes financial abundance when handled with wisdom and responsibility.

Wealth Is A Blessing From God

Wealth can mean different things to different people. For some, it might mean having a lot of money; for others, it could mean having a stable home, good health, or supportive relationships. However, the Bible teaches us that all wealth comes from God. This understanding can change how we view and use our resources. In Deuteronomy 8:18, we read, "*But thou shalt remember the LORD thy God: for it is he that giveth thee power to get wealth, that he may establish his covenant which he sware unto thy fathers, as it is this day.*" God gives us the ability to earn and manage wealth. It's essential to recognize that our skills, talents, and opportunities are all gifts from God. Without Him, we wouldn't have what we have. When we see wealth as a gift from God, we realize it is part of His larger plan. God gives us wealth to enjoy and fulfill His promises and purposes. This perspective reminds us to be grateful and humble, understanding that everything we have is ultimately a blessing from God.

Seeing wealth as a blessing also means considering how we use it. Wealth should not be seen merely as something to brag about or use only for ourselves. Instead, it is a resource that God has entrusted to us so we can honor Him and help others. Proverbs 10:22, "The blessing of the LORD, it maketh rich, and he addeth no sorrow with it." This verse teaches us that true wealth comes from God's blessing. When we pursue wealth with the right heart and align our desires with God's will, we can experience a kind of prosperity that brings joy and peace. When we understand that wealth is a blessing from God, it changes how we think about money. We stop seeing it as something we must chase after at any cost. Instead, we can view it as a tool to serve God and others. This perspective helps us to be more generous and compassionate, as we recognize that what we have is not solely for our benefit. One of the critical responsibilities that come with wealth is the ability to bless others. We are called to use our resources to help those in need, support our communities, and further God's work. 2 Corinthians 9:7, "Every man according as he purposeth in his heart, so let him give; not grudgingly, or of necessity: for God loveth a cheerful giver." This means that God loves when we give willingly and joyfully. Sharing our wealth reflects God's love and generosity to the world. It is an opportunity to be a blessing to others; in doing so, we find fulfillment and joy. When our wealth comes from God's blessing, it brings peace and contentment. We don't have to worry about competing with others or fearing losing what we have. Instead, we can trust that God will provide for our needs. Philippians 4:19 reminds us, "But my God shall supply all your need according to his riches in glory by Christ Jesus." This promise assures us that God will take care of us.

God Desires Prosperity For His People

When we think about God, we often focus on His love, grace, and guidance. However, it's equally important to understand that God desires prosperity for us spiritually and in our physical and financial lives. This prosperity allows us to lead fulfilling lives and to serve others effectively. God has plans that are good and filled with hope. He desires peace and stability for us, which often includes financial well-being. We can find comfort in knowing God wants us to thrive when we trust His plans. God's desire for our prosperity means He wants us to have the resources to live and help others. Financial stability can free us to focus on our purpose, serve others, and contribute to the advancement of His Kingdom. Abraham is one of the earliest examples of this, and he is known for his great faith. Genesis 13:2 says, "Abram was rich in cattle, *silver, and gold."* Abraham's wealth was a sign of God's favor. He used his resources to fulfill God's purposes, including helping others and building a nation. Job, another significant example, is Job. After enduring severe suffering and loss, Job remained faithful to God. In Job 42:10, God blessed Job with *"twice as much as he had before."* This shows God's ability to restore and that true prosperity can come after trials, reinforcing the idea that God rewards faithfulness. These examples indicate that God's blessings often include material wealth. However, it's essential to remember that wealth should be seen as a tool for good rather than an end goal.

Understanding that God desires our prosperity leads us to the responsibility of stewardship. This means managing the resources God gives us wisely and faithfully. We should seek to honor God with our wealth, using it to bless others, support our communities, and further His Kingdom. Luke 16:10, *"He that is faithful in that which is least is faithful also in much."* Being responsible with small resources leads to greater responsibilities. When we prove ourselves trustworthy with our finances, God can entrust us with more blessings. Financial stability allows us to focus on God's work without the distractions of economic stress. It enables us to give generously, support ministries, and serve those in need. When our needs are met, we can focus on helping others and spreading God's love. Moreover, having financial security can allow us to share our blessings with struggling people. 2 Corinthians 9:8, *"And God can make all grace abound toward you; that ye, always having all sufficiency in all things, may abound to every good work."* God provides us with enough to fulfill His work and to bless others. While God desires prosperity for us, it's essential to maintain a balanced perspective. Wealth is not the ultimate goal; it's a means to fulfill God's purposes. When we pursue wealth for selfish reasons, it can lead to greed and dissatisfaction. However, when we align our financial pursuits with God's will, we can experience true prosperity that brings joy and peace.

While God desires prosperity for His children, it's crucial to understand that with wealth comes great responsibility. The Bible teaches that how we manage our resources reflects our relationship with God and our understanding of His purposes for our lives. Luke 12:48, *"For unto whomsoever much is given, of him shall be much required."* When God blesses us with wealth, He expects us to use it wisely. We must care for ourselves and consider how our wealth can serve God and others. We are called to be good stewards of what we have received. This means managing our finances with wisdom, integrity, and an eye towards God's purposes. It's about understanding that our resources are not solely for our enjoyment but are meant to fulfill God's plans. Wealth can easily lead to selfishness and greed if we are not careful. 1 Timothy 6:10, *"For the love of money is the root of all evil."* This verse is often misunderstood; it does not claim that money itself is evil but rather that the love of money—greed—can lead to harmful actions and decisions. When we prioritize money above God, it can become an idol. We start choosing based on what will benefit us financially rather than what will honor God or serve others. This shift in focus can lead to destructive behavior, such as dishonesty, exploitation, and neglecting the needs of those around us.

In response to the responsibility that comes with wealth, the Bible emphasizes the importance of generosity. When we prosper, we must ask ourselves how to use our resources to bless others. Acts of generosity reflect a heart aligned with God's purposes and demonstrate our understanding that everything we have ultimately comes from Him. When we share our blessings, we help others and open ourselves up to receiving more blessings from God. As we consider our responsibility, we should focus on how our wealth can support ministry efforts and build the Kingdom of God. This might involve donating to churches, missions, and charities that align with God's work. In 2 Corinthians 9:7, Paul encourages believers by saying, "Every man according as he purposeth in his heart, so let him give; not grudgingly, or of necessity: for God loveth a cheerful giver." Giving should come from a joyful heart, recognizing that our contributions can significantly impact the lives of others and further God's mission on Earth.

The Principle Of Seedtime And Harvest

One of the most powerful ideas in the Bible regarding prosperity is the principle of seed time and harvest. This principle is about the relationship between what we give and what we receive. It teaches us that our actions—mainly how we handle our resources—have significant consequences. Galatians 6:7, *"Be not deceived; God is not mocked: for whatsoever a man soweth, that shall he also reap."* As farmers plant seeds and expect a harvest, our actions will produce results. We can expect blessings in return if we choose to be generous and use our resources to bless others. This principle of sowing and reaping is not just about finances; it applies to all areas of life. When we invest our time, energy, and resources into good deeds and helping others, we create a cycle of kindness and generosity that often comes back to us unexpectedly. Jesus emphasized this principle of generosity in Luke 6:38, where He says, *"Give, and it shall be given unto you; good measure, pressed down, and shaken together, and running over, shall men give into your bosom. For with the same measure that ye mete withal it shall be measured to you again."* Here, Jesus assures us that when we give, we will receive in abundance. The imagery of "pressed down and shaken together" suggests that the blessings we receive will be overflowing, often exceeding our expectations. This teaching encourages us to be open-handed with our resources. It reminds us that generosity blesses others and leads to our abundance. When we give freely, God ensures that our needs are met in ways we might not foresee.

The principle of seed time and harvest is closely tied to stewardship. God expects us to manage our resources wisely and to use them to sow into the lives of others. Contributing to the church's work helps spread the Gospel and provide for those in need. When we give to our church, we participate in something greater than ourselves. Providing for those who are less fortunate is a direct way to show God's love. Proverbs 19:17, *"He that hath pity upon the poor lendeth unto the LORD, and that which he hath given will he pay him again."* When we help others, we are lending to God. Investing in ministries that align with our values and God's mission can have a lasting impact. This includes supporting missionaries, community outreach programs, and other initiatives to spread hope and help those in need.

God's Covenant Of Provision

In the Old Testament, God made a specific covenant with the

Israelites, assuring them of His provision as long as they obeyed His commandments. Deuteronomy 28:11-12, *"And the LORD shall make thee plenteous in goods, in the fruit of thy body, and in the fruit of thy cattle, and the fruit of thy ground... The LORD shall open unto thee his good treasure, the heaven to give the rain unto thy land in his season, and to bless all the work of thine hand."* God will provide abundantly for His people. The phrase "plenteous in goods" indicates that their needs—both physical and material— would be met. The blessings promised include fruitful harvests, healthy families, and successful labor. God's intention was clear: if they followed Him faithfully, they would experience His generous provision in every aspect of their lives. This covenant of provision does not end with the Old Testament. In the New Testament, we see God's promise of provision continuing in a new light. Philippians 4:19, *"But my God shall supply all your need according to his riches in glory by Christ Jesus."* We are part of God's family, and He promises to supply all our needs. It emphasizes that God's provision is not limited to physical necessities but encompasses all aspects of our lives—spiritual, emotional, and material. *"According to his riches in glory"* highlights the abundance and richness of God's resources, suggesting that His supply is more than sufficient to meet our needs.

God's promise of provision is linked to our trust in Him and willingness to follow His commandments. Just as the Israelites were called to obey God's laws, we, too, must seek to live according to His will. Trusting in God's provision means believing He will care for our needs, even when circumstances seem challenging. God's provision may not always come in the way or time we expect. Just as the Israelites relied on God for rain in its season, we must be patient and trust His timing. It's essential to recognize and express gratitude for the provision we receive. Acknowledging God's hand in our lives encourages a thankful heart and fosters a deeper relationship with Him. We should regularly thank Him for His blessings, both big and small. As God blesses us, we are called to share those blessings with others. This can be through acts of kindness, generosity, and support to those in need. When we share what we have, we become conduits of God's provision, reflecting His love and care for others.

Wealth For Kingdom Purposes

Wealth is often seen as a means of personal comfort, security, or even societal status. However, from a biblical perspective, wealth holds a more profound purpose—it is a tool for advancing God's Kingdom. God blesses us not merely for our benefit but so that we can be a blessing to others and fulfill His work on earth. 2 Corinthians 9:8, *"And God can make all grace abound toward you; that ye, always having all sufficiency in all things, may abound to every good work."* God's grace provides us with everything we need —not just for our lives, but so we can abound in good works. The phrase "every good work" signifies various acts of kindness, charity, and ministry that can positively impact the world. God blesses us abundantly so we can meet the needs of others and contribute to the spread of the Gospel—our approach to financial stewardship changes when we recognize that wealth is intended for Kingdom purposes.

One of the most direct ways to use our resources is by supporting churches, missionaries, and various ministries. Our financial contributions enable them to carry out their work, whether feeding the hungry, providing shelter, or spreading the Gospel. When we give generously, we participate in God's mission and help reach people with His love. Wealth offers opportunities to assist those in need within our communities. Acts of kindness, such as donating to local charities or helping families in distress, demonstrate God's love in practical ways. By being sensitive to the needs around us, we can use our resources to lift others and make a significant difference in their lives. Wealth can also be used to foster relationships within the Christian community. This might include hosting gatherings, supporting church events, or even offering financial help to fellow believers. Building a solid community reflects God's love and unity, creating an environment where faith can thrive. As believers, we are called to be advocates for justice and mercy. Wealth allows us to support organizations that fight for the marginalized, speak out against injustice, and bring positive societal change. Using our resources to stand up for the oppressed aligns our actions with God's heart for justice.

Viewing wealth as a means for Kingdom purposes shifts our focus from temporary gains to eternal impact. The resources we accumulate in this life will not follow us into eternity. However, the lives we touch and the seeds we plant through acts of kindness, generosity, and support for God's work will have lasting consequences. Matthew 6:19-20, *"Lay not up for yourselves treasures upon earth, where moth and rust doth corrupt, and where thieves break through and steal: But lay up for yourselves treasures in heaven, where neither moth nor rust doth corrupt, and where thieves do not break through nor steal."* By prioritizing Kingdom purposes over earthly possessions, we store treasures in heaven— where they cannot be taken away. When used wisely, our wealth becomes a powerful instrument for good that echoes into eternity.

CHAPTER 2

STEWARDSHIP: MANAGING GOD'S RESOURCES WISELY

Stewardship is a foundational concept in the Bible that teaches us how to view our resources—money, time, talents, and even relationships. It emphasizes that we are not owners of these resources but rather managers entrusted by God to use them wisely. The Bible makes it abundantly clear that everything we have belongs to God. In Psalm 24:1, we read: "The earth is the LORD's, and the fulness thereof; the world, and they that dwell therein." All the wealth, possessions, and even the people we interact with belong to God. We are simply caretakers of what He has entrusted to us. Recognizing this truth can profoundly change how we approach our lives and decisions regarding our resources.

One of the most explicit stewardship illustrations is the parable of the talents in Matthew 25:14-30. In this story, Jesus describes a master who goes on a journey and entrusts his wealth to his servants. He gives each servant different amounts of money, called "talents," according to their ability. The first two servants invest their talents and successfully increase their master's wealth. When the master returns, he praises and rewards them for their faithfulness and good management. However, the third servant, who received one talent, buried it out of fear and did nothing with it. When the master returns, he rebukes this servant, saying he should have at least invested it to earn interest. As a result, the talent is taken away from him. God expects us to use what He has given us, whether minor or grand, and increase it for His glory. The focus is not solely on the amount we are given but on how we manage and grow those resources.

Understanding our role as managers rather than owners changes our perspective on wealth and resources. As managers, we have a responsibility to use our resources wisely. This includes making thoughtful decisions about how we spend our money, the time we invest in others, and how we use our talents and abilities. We are called to view our money, abilities, and opportunities as tools to accomplish God's work. This means that every financial decision we make, every skill we use, and every moment we spend can be directed toward fulfilling God's purposes. A proper understanding of stewardship leads to generosity. When we recognize that our resources are not ours but belong to God, we are more willing to share with others and support the work of the Kingdom.

As managers, we will ultimately be held accountable for using what God has given us. In the parable, the servants were called to give an account of their stewardship. Likewise, we will be called to account for how we have managed our resources. The key to stewardship is recognizing that we are not owners but managers of what belongs to God. This mindset shifts our focus from accumulating wealth for personal gain to using it for God's purposes. It encourages us to ask: "How can I use my finances to bless others and support ministry?" "How can I develop my skills and talents to serve God and my community?" "How can I use my time to reflect God's love and make a positive impact in the lives of others?"

Faithfulness In Small Things

One of the essential principles of stewardship is being faithful to what we have, regardless of the amount. The Bible teaches us that how we manage small things can influence our ability to handle more significant responsibilities. Luke 16:10, *"He that is faithful in that which is least is faithful also in much: and he that is unjust in the least is unjust also in much."* If we are trustworthy with small amounts of money or resources, God will entrust us with more. However, if we are careless or wasteful with what we have, we show that we are not ready to handle greater responsibilities. Faithfulness starts with trustworthiness. Being diligent and responsible with small tasks reflects our character and prepares us for more significant opportunities. For example, if someone is given a small allowance and uses it wisely, they may be trusted with a more substantial sum later. We must recognize that every resource we have—time, money, or talent—matters to God. Small acts of faithfulness in managing what we have can lead to more significant blessings.

Being a good steward involves making wise decisions with our finances. Creating and sticking to a budget is fundamental to managing money wisely. A budget helps us track income and expenses, ensuring we live within our means and prioritize necessary expenses. It allows us to wisely allocate resources toward savings, charity, and investments. Setting aside money for future needs, such as emergencies, education, or retirement, shows foresight and responsibility. Proverbs 21:20 "There is a treasure to be desired and oil in the dwelling of the wise, but a foolish man spendeth it up." The wise person saves and prepares for the future, while the foolish person wastes what they have without consideration. Being cautious about taking on debt is another vital aspect of financial stewardship. At the same time, some debt may be necessary (like a mortgage or student loans, so we should avoid accumulating debt for non-essential purchases. This helps us maintain financial stability and frees us to give generously.

Cultivating gratitude for what we already have can shift our perspective and lead to wise spending. Recognizing that our resources are gifts from God encourages us to be more thoughtful and less wasteful. Instead of merely saving money, we can look for ways to invest our resources. This could mean investing money into a savings account with interest, investing in education to improve our skills, or supporting businesses and ministries aligning with our values. Faithfulness in small things often creates a ripple effect in our lives. When we are responsible for what we have, we build a reputation for reliability, leading to more opportunities in life and work. People notice when someone is trustworthy, and this can lead to new jobs, promotions, or partnerships. Additionally, being faithful to small things can inspire others to do the same. Our actions can encourage friends and family to be wise with their resources, creating a community that values stewardship and generosity.

Stewardship Of Time And Talents

Stewardship extends beyond managing money and encompasses how we use our time and talents. God has uniquely equipped each of us with abilities and opportunities, and He expects us to utilize them to serve others and build His Kingdom. 1 Peter 4:10, *"As every man hath received the gift, even so, minister the same one to another, as good stewards of the manifold grace of God."* Each of us has received unique gifts from God. Whether our talents lie in teaching, music, service, or hospitality, we are called to use these gifts to bless others and glorify God. The first step in being a good steward of our talents is to identify what they are. This might involve self-reflection, prayer, or even seeking feedback from others.

God has given us these gifts for a purpose, and understanding them helps us find our place in His plan. Once we identify our gifts, we should look for opportunities to serve. This could mean volunteering in the church, helping a neighbor, or mentoring someone in need. By using our talents to benefit others, we fulfill God's command to love our neighbors and positively impact our communities. Stewardship of our talents also involves encouraging others to use their gifts. This creates a supportive environment where everyone feels valued and empowered to contribute. We can uplift those around us by recognizing their abilities and encouraging them to serve.

In addition to talents, time is another precious resource God has entrusted us. Ephesians 5:16, *"Redeeming the time, because the days are evil."* To redeem our time, we must prioritize activities that align with God's purpose for our lives. This includes praying, studying Scripture, serving others, and fulfilling our responsibilities in work and family life. Being a good steward of time also means learning to say "no" to activities that do not contribute to our well-being or spiritual growth. By setting healthy boundaries, we can create space for what truly matters and avoid burnout.

In our fast-paced world, it's easy to get distracted. Being present at the moment—whether with family, friends or in prayer—allows us to engage with those around us and deepen our relationships comprehensively. Regularly assessing how we spend our time can help us identify areas for improvement. Are we dedicating time to spiritual growth? Are we serving in our community? This evaluation helps us adjust our schedules to better align with God's priorities. Finding time for hobbies and relaxation is essential, but we should also consider how to use our free time for God's work. Whether volunteering, participating in church activities, or mentoring others, even our leisure time can be an opportunity to serve.

Financial Stewardship: Managing Wealth With Integrity

Financial stewardship is a practical way to apply stewardship principles to our wealth. The Bible provides clear guidance on how to manage our finances in a way that honors God and reflects His values. Here are fundamental principles for effective financial stewardship: One of the first principles is to avoid debt whenever possible. Proverbs 22:7 *"The rich ruleth over the poor, and the borrower is servant to the lender."* At the same time, there may be circumstances where borrowing is necessary (such as for a home or education, we should strive to borrow responsibly and minimize debt to maintain financial freedom. Here are some strategies. Make a budget that reflects your income and expenses. Avoid lifestyle inflation and make choices that prioritize your financial health. Instead of impulsively buying on credit, save for major purchases. It will help you avoid unnecessary debt and teach you the value of patience and preparation. Before borrowing, consider other options like saving or seeking assistance. Often, there are creative solutions that can help you avoid debt altogether.

Saving For The Future

Proverbs 6:6-8 teaches us an important lesson about preparation and diligence: *"Go to the ant, thou sluggard; consider her ways, and be wise: which having no guide, overseer, or ruler, provideth her meat in the summer, and gathereth her food in the harvest."* The ant instinctively prepares for the future, gathering resources during times of plenty to ensure survival during leaner times. This biblical principle encourages us to save wisely for future needs.

One of the first steps in financial planning is creating an emergency fund. It is recommended to save three to six months' living expenses to protect yourself from unexpected events such as job loss, medical emergencies, or sudden repairs. Just as the ant prepares during times of harvest, saving during stable times can provide a safety net when challenges arise. Whether you're saving for retirement, a child's education, or a significant purchase, setting specific savings goals helps you stay focused and motivated. Having a clear target can measure your progress and maintain discipline in your savings journey. Consider setting up automatic transfers to your savings account to make saving easier. By treating your savings like a bill that must be paid, you're more likely to save consistently and avoid the temptation to spend. Automation takes the guesswork out of saving, allowing you to build up your savings without thinking about it. Just as the ant prepares for future needs, we, too, should be diligent in saving for unexpected events and future goals. By setting aside some of our resources, we demonstrate wisdom and stewardship, ensuring we are prepared for whatever lies ahead.

Accountability To God

Being accountable to God means we are responsible for how we live our lives and use what He has given us, such as our time, talents, money, and opportunities. We will one day stand before God and explain how we managed all these gifts. Romans 14:12: *"Every one of us shall give an account of himself to God."* It means we are all responsible for how we live and our choices. God has given us many things in life—our abilities, time, money, relationships, and opportunities. He expects us to use them wisely. Just like a manager takes care of a business for the owner, we are called to care for what God has given us because everything belongs to Him. We must remember that one day, we will explain to God how we used these gifts. When we understand that we will give an account to God, it changes how we live. We are more careful about how we spend our time and money and treat others. It reminds us that every choice matters, and we should always ask, "Am I using what God has given me the right way?"

Being accountable to God isn't just money or big decisions; it includes everything. Everything matters to God, from how we treat people, how we work, how we spend our free time, and how we help others. Because we are accountable to God, we should always seek His wisdom before making decisions. It can be done through prayer, reading the Bible, and listening to His guidance. By doing so, we can make the right choices that honor Him. When we know we are accountable to God, it helps us stay responsible. Just like we do our best at work when we know the boss will check on us, knowing that God will one day ask us how we live makes us more serious about using our time, talents, and money wisely.

Accountability pushes us to work hard and be faithful in whatever we are doing. Whether it's in our job, our relationships, or in helping others, knowing that God sees everything encourages us to do our best. Life is full of distractions and temporary things, but knowing that we are accountable to God reminds us to focus on what matters. It helps us think about eternal values, such as love, kindness, generosity, and helping others, rather than just chasing after things like money, fame, or success. We are not just living for today but for eternity. Our accountability to God doesn't end with our time on earth; it affects our eternity. Jesus talks about rewards in Heaven for those who live faithfully on earth. It should encourage us to live with an eternal perspective—choosing things that honor God and have lasting value rather than just things that bring temporary pleasure.

Lessons From The Parable Of The Talents

TThe parable of the talents in Matthew 25:14-30 provides a powerful message about stewardship, responsibility, and accountability. In this parable, a master entrusts three servants with different amounts of money (called talents before leaving on a long journey. Upon his return, he asks for an account of how they used what was given. Stewardship is more than just holding on to what we have; it's about using our resources wisely and productively. The first two servants doubled the money they were given, showing they actively worked to improve and grow what was entrusted to them. The third servant, however, did nothing —he buried his talent out of fear and laziness. God expects us to be active with what He gives us, whether money, talents, or opportunities. We should not sit back but use our gifts to impact others and His Kingdom positively. The master gave each servant a different amount of money based on their abilities. The two servants who received five and two talents doubled their amounts, proving their faithfulness. The third servant, who received one talent, failed because he didn't try to do anything with it. God knows our abilities and gives us responsibilities based on what we can handle. He doesn't expect the same results from everyone, but He does expect faithfulness. It's not about how much we have but how we use what we've been given.

The servant who buried his talent faced severe consequences. The master called him "wicked and slothful," he was punished for failing to act. It shows that neglecting what God gives us, whether out of fear, laziness, or selfishness, is unacceptable. There are real consequences for failing to be good stewards of God's gifts. We are accountable for how we use our time, talents, and resources, and there is a cost to inaction or laziness. God wants us to make the most of the opportunities He provides. The parable shows that God expects growth and increase. The master was pleased with the two servants who had multiplied their talents, and He rewarded them with even more responsibilities. The unfaithful servant not only lost his talent but also gave it to the servant who had been most productive. God wants us to grow and develop the gifts and resources He entrusts us. When we do, we are blessed with even more excellent opportunities to serve Him. The unfaithful servant claimed he feared the master's strictness, so he did nothing with his talent. His fear led to inactivity, and this excuse did not save him from the master's anger. Fear should not hold us back from using what God has given us. Instead of letting fear paralyze us, we should trust in God's wisdom and guidance as we move forward in faith. God desires us to act, even if we fear making mistakes.

Stewardship As Worship

Stewardship is not just a matter of managing resources but a way of expressing worship to God. Everything we have—our time, talents, and finances—comes from God, and when we manage these resources well, we honor Him and acknowledge His role as the ultimate owner of all things. Colossians 3:23-24, *"And whatsoever ye do, do it heartily, as to the Lord, and not unto men; knowing that of the Lord ye shall receive the reward of the inheritance: for ye serve the Lord Christ."* Our actions should be done to please God, not just for human recognition.

Stewardship becomes worship when we manage our resources to serve God. When we give to others, use our talents, or make financial decisions, it's not just about the action itself but the heart behind it. By doing these things with a desire to honor God, we elevate the ordinary tasks of life into acts of service to Him. Every decision we make with our resources can be a form of worship when we do it to honor God. Even small actions, like budgeting or giving to a cause, are opportunities to serve God from the heart.

The way we manage our resources reflects what we value most. If we prioritize God in our stewardship, it shows that our love for Him is genuine. When we are generous, it reflects God's generosity. When we are wise, it shows that we are following His guidance. In this way, stewardship is a mirror of our relationship with God. Stewardship is a reflection of our love for God. By managing our resources wisely, we show that we trust His provision and care more about His Kingdom than material wealth. In every financial decision, whether big or small, we must seek to align our choices with God's will. It means turning to prayer and Scripture for guidance and asking how our choices can further God's purposes. Are we using our finances to bless others? Are we using our talents to serve the church or our community? By putting God first, we make our decisions an act of worship. Prioritizing God in our financial decisions means asking how our choices can serve Him. Whether saving, investing, or giving, we should always consider how our actions can glorify God and build His Kingdom.

Generosity is a critical component of stewardship that illustrates our worship. When we give to others, support ministry, or contribute to charitable causes, we are not just fulfilling obligations but worshiping God through our actions. *Proverbs 11:25, "The liberal soul shall be made fat: and he that watereth shall be watered also himself."* God also blesses us as we bless others, creating a cycle of worship and provision—our attitude in giving matters. When we give joyfully, it becomes an act of worship rather than a mere transaction. Managing our time and talents also involves excellence. Working diligently and serving others with our abilities honors God. Ephesians 2:10, *"For we are his workmanship, created in Christ Jesus unto good works, which God hath before ordained that we should walk in them."* Recognizing our skills and talents as gifts from God leads us to use them for His glory and the benefit of others. Every aspect of our lives can be an act of worship when done in His name.

CHAPTER 3

GENEROSITY: THE HEART OF KINGDOM IMPACT

G enerosity lies in the very nature of God. He is the ultimate giver, and His abundant love for us is shown through His generous provision. John 3:16. "For God so loved the world, that he gave his only begotten Son, that whosoever believeth in him should not perish, but have everlasting life." The greatest gift ever given—God's only Son, Jesus Christ. Through this ultimate sacrifice, God provided a way for us to receive salvation and eternal life. This act of love sets a standard for our generosity; it teaches us to give freely, sacrificially, and with love. God's giving was driven by love and purpose, not just about meeting a need. As Christians, we are called to reflect this kind of giving. When we give, we should consider how our gifts can express love and support to others. God did not wait for us to earn His love or merit His grace; He gave freely. Our generosity should mirror this principle, allowing us to give without conditions or expectations—this kind of providing fosters a spirit of kindness and community.

James 1:17, *"Every good gift and every perfect gift is from above, and cometh down from the Father of lights, with whom is no variableness, neither shadow of turning."* All good things in our lives are gifts from God. Recognizing Him as the source of our blessings shapes our attitude toward giving. When we offer, we acknowledge that everything we have comes from God. This awareness helps us be less possessive and more willing to share, knowing God provides for our needs. Understanding that our resources are a gift from God inspires us to respond with gratitude. Generosity becomes an overflow of thankfulness for what we have received, compelling us to bless others the same way we have been. When we practice generosity, we imitate God's nature. This reflection of His character impacts those we help and strengthens our relationship with God. We grow closer to Him as we align our hearts with His desire to give and bless others.

The Heart Of Generosity: Giving With Love

Generosity is more than just an action; it reflects the heart. When we give, God is not just looking at the amount we offer but at the attitude and motivation behind it. 2 Corinthians 9:7, *"Every man according as he purposeth in his heart, so let him give; not grudgingly, or of necessity: for God loveth a cheerful giver."* Giving should come from a place of love, gratitude, and willingness, not from pressure or obligation. God calls us to give thoughtfully and with intention. It's not about giving because we feel we have to but because we want to. When we provide purposefully, we consciously decide to bless others out of the abundance that God has given us. This kind of giving reflects a heart aligned with God's will and Generosity. Giving should come from a place of love and thoughtfulness, not from guilt or compulsion. When we provide intentionally, we reflect the care and purposefulness of God Himself.

God loves a cheerful giver because cheerful giving reflects His character. When we give joyfully, we mirror the generosity that God shows us every day. His love for us is not forced; in the same way, our giving should flow naturally from our hearts. Giving with joy makes generosity a form of worship, bringing delight to

God and ourselves. Giving is meant to be a joyful act that reflects God's nature. When we give cheerfully, we are not only fulfilling God's command, but we are also entering into a more profound joy and connection with Him. When we give out of love rather than duty, we experience freedom. No longer is generosity a burden; it becomes a source of joy and fulfillment. This freedom comes from understanding that everything we have is a gift from God, and we simply pass on the blessings we've received. Giving from this perspective frees us from the pressure of obligation and allows us to enjoy the act of blessing others. Generosity becomes a delight when it's motivated by love. When we are free from the weight of obligation, we can give joyfully and experience the happiness of helping others.

Generosity driven by love does more than just meet physical needs; it reveals God's character through our actions. When we give from a place of love, we display God's love and nature to others. Our giving is a mirror of God's love for us. Just as God gives us abundantly—whether through grace, provision, or spiritual blessings—our generosity becomes an extension of that love to others. When we give freely and without expectation, we show selfless love to those around us. Generosity allows us to reflect the love of God. We demonstrate His boundless love and care for humanity when we give without hesitation. Generosity has a way of building relationships and fostering a sense of community. Acts of kindness, mainly when driven by love, create stronger bonds between individuals and groups. When we give, we are not just providing resources; we share the joy of connecting with others. This creates an atmosphere of mutual support and encouragement, reminding us that we are part of a more extensive community rooted in love. Generosity helps us form joyful and meaningful connections with others. It strengthens our relationships, builds trust, and fosters a sense of unity and belonging within the community.

Acts 20:35, *"It is more blessed to give than to receive."* Giving is not just about helping others; it also brings personal satisfaction and spiritual rewards. One of the greatest joys of giving is knowing that we are helping others. When we give—whether it's our time, money, or talents—we become vessels of God's blessings. By supporting someone in need, we bring hope, comfort, and encouragement to their lives. Knowing that we can make a difference, even in small ways, fills our hearts with a sense of purpose and joy. Giving blesses both the giver and the receiver. It allows us to be part of God's plan to care for and uplift others, which brings us joy and satisfaction. There is a deep sense of fulfillment that comes from giving. While receiving can bring temporary happiness, the joy of giving often has a lasting impact. When we see the positive effects of our generosity, we feel a sense of accomplishment and purpose. This feeling is usually far greater than the happiness of getting something for ourselves. The joy of giving lies in knowing that we are contributing to something bigger than ourselves. It provides us with a sense of fulfillment that goes beyond material gain. We actively participate in God's work of love, care, and service when we give. Generosity is a tangible way to live out our faith and show our commitment to God's Kingdom. By sharing what we have, we become part of God's mission to reach others with His love and provision. This brings a deep spiritual joy as we align our actions with God's heart. Giving is a form of worship, reflecting our desire to serve God and others. It brings us closer to God and allows us to be part of His ongoing work.

Generosity As An Act Of Faith

Generosity is not just a good deed but a profound act of faith. When we give, we demonstrate our trust in God's provision and acknowledge that all we have ultimately comes from Him. When we give generously, we show that we believe God will continue to meet our needs. This principle is beautifully captured in Proverbs 11:24-25, *"There is that scattereth, and yet increaseth; and there is that withholdeth more than is meet, but it tendeth to* poverty. *The liberal soul shall be made fat: and he that watereth shall also be watered."* Those who give freely often end up receiving more. This challenges the common mindset that hoarding resources ensures security. In God's economy, generosity leads to abundance. Withholding out of fear can lead to scarcity, while open-handedness fosters trust in God's provision. Generosity acts as a declaration of faith, showing that we believe God will provide for our needs, even when we give away what we have. Mark 12:41-44, *"And Jesus sat over against the treasury, and beheld how the people cast money into the treasury: and many rich cast in much. And there came a certain poor widow, who threw in two mites, making a farthing. And he called unto him his disciples, and saith unto them, Verily I say unto you, That this poor widow hath cast more in, than all they which have cast into the treasury: For all, they did cast in of their abundance; but she of her want did cast in all that she had, even all her living."* The widow's two small coins were insignificant in monetary terms, yet Jesus praised her gift because she gave all she had. Her generosity stemmed from deep faith, showing that God values the heart behind the gift rather than its size. The widow exemplifies sacrificial giving—she gave out of her need, trusting God completely. This challenges us to consider our giving habits. Are we giving out of abundance, or are we willing to sacrifice for the sake of others? God honors the heart of faith behind our giving. The widow's act was a testament to her trust in God, and Jesus highlighted her as a model of true generosity.

Generosity Brings Blessings

Generosity is not just about fulfilling a duty—it's a gateway to experiencing God's blessings. The Bible teaches that when we give with an open heart, the giver and receiver are blessed. These blessings come in many forms, from spiritual growth to material provision. Luke 6:38 says, *"Give, and it shall be given unto you; good measure, pressed down, shaken together, and running over, shall men give into your bosom. With the same measure that ye mete withal, it shall be measured to you again."* When we give generously, we set into motion a cycle of blessing. Just as a farmer reaps more than he sows, the same applies to our generosity—what we give returns to us in multiplied ways. The imagery of "good measure, pressed down, and shaken together" paints a picture of God's abundant provision, showing that He rewards giving beyond our expectations. The blessings we receive from generosity often come in unexpected ways. These might not always be financial; they can also include emotional joy, peace, spiritual growth, or relational blessings. God works in mysterious ways to return the kindness we show to others. Malachi 3:10, *"Bring ye all the tithes into the storehouse, that there may be meat in mine house, and prove me now herewith, saith the LORD of hosts, if I will not open you the windows of heaven, and pour you out a blessing, that there shall not be room enough to receive it."* God challenges us to test His faithfulness through our giving. He promises that when we bring our tithes and offerings, He will open the windows of heaven and pour out such abundant blessings that we won't have enough room to contain them. This shows that God delights in rewarding generosity and that our giving is never unnoticed. God's blessings are never scarce. He can provide for us in ways that far exceed our giving. By honoring God with our finances, time, and talents, we can trust that He will meet our needs and bless us in ways overflowing into every area of our lives. Generosity opens the door to both spiritual and material blessings. When we give, we reflect God's heart and align ourselves with His principles of love and kindness. In return, we experience His abundant provision now and in eternity. Through giving, we experience the true joy of living a life that mirrors God's generosity. While the blessings of generosity are apparent, it's essential to reflect on the reasons we give. Our primary motivation should come from our love for God and our desire to obey Him. When we give cheerfully, we recognize all God has done for us and respond joyfully. It's not about fulfilling an obligation or seeking recognition but expressing our appreciation for His blessings. Giving also shows our faith in God's ability to meet our needs. When we release our resources, we demonstrate our belief that God controls us and knows what is best for us. Trusting God means believing that He will take care of us, even when we step out in faith to give. This act of trust deepens our relationship with Him and encourages us to rely on His provision.

Generosity As A Kingdom Investment

Generosity is not just about meeting immediate needs; it's a powerful way to invest in God's Kingdom. When we give to support ministries, missionaries, churches, and those in need, we actively advance God's work on Earth. Matthew 6:19-20, *"Lay not up for yourselves treasures upon earth, where moth and rust doth corrupt, and where thieves break through and steal: but lay up for yourselves treasures in heaven, where neither moth nor rust doth corrupt, and where thieves do not break through nor steal."* Material possessions can wear out, become outdated, or even be stolen. Instead of focusing solely on accumulating wealth and possessions, Jesus encourages us to invest in what truly matters— things of eternal value. When we give generously, we essentially store up treasures in heaven, where they are safe and everlasting. Every act of generosity contributes to God's Kingdom's work. Whether supporting a local church, funding a missionary, or helping those in need, our contributions help spread the Gospel message and transform lives. Each donation, no matter how small, helps create a more significant impact, supporting efforts that can lead to eternal changes in the hearts of individuals. These acts of kindness have a ripple effect, creating opportunities for others to experience God's love and grace. When we give, we become partners in God's mission. We help support projects that spread the Gospel, feed the hungry, provide shelter, and heal the broken. This gives our lives a greater purpose, as we know we are part of something bigger than ourselves. While our generosity blesses others, it also brings rewards for us in heaven. The Bible teaches that God sees our hearts and our willingness to give. These eternal rewards can take many forms, including spiritual fulfillment and the joy of seeing lives changed by our contributions. Philippians 4:17, "Not because I desire a gift: but I desire fruit that may abound to your account." Paul acknowledges that while he appreciates the support he receives, his greater desire is for the spiritual fruit that comes from their generosity. When we give to support the work of the Gospel, we participate in something much more significant than ourselves; we contribute to advancing God's Kingdom. This means that our giving becomes a part of God's mission to bring hope, love, and salvation to the world. Each contribution is a seed sown in faith, leading to an abundant harvest of transformed lives. Supporting the work of the Gospel brings eternal rewards. When we invest in the lives of others through our generosity, we are meeting immediate needs and participating in God's plan for redemption and restoration. Our giving can change hearts and lives, resulting in eternal impact. Each act of kindness, whether through financial support, time, or resources, helps build God's Kingdom on Earth and contributes to spreading His message of love and grace.

Generosity As A Witness To The World

Generosity is not just a personal virtue; it is a powerful witness that reflects the love of Christ to those around us. When Christians give freely and generously, they demonstrate the transformative impact of faith in action. Acts 4:32-35, "*And the multitude of them that believed were of one heart and one soul: neither said any of them that ought of the things which he possessed was his own, but they had all things common. And with great power, the apostles witnessed the resurrection of the Lord Jesus: and great grace was upon them all. Neither was there any among them that lacked: for as many as were possessors of lands or houses sold them, and brought the prices of the things that were sold, and laid them down at the apostles' feet: and distribution was made unto every man according as he had need.*" Their willingness to share their possessions and care for one another created a strong bond that set them apart from the world. This radical generosity attracted others to their faith, showing that love in action can lead to spiritual awakening. The early church's actions were not just about meeting needs; they were a testimony to the power of Christ's resurrection. Their generosity illustrated the impact of the Gospel on their lives, making them credible witnesses to the truth of Jesus Christ.

When we care for those in need and support individuals in crisis, we demonstrate God's love in practical ways. Whether through food drives, financial support, or volunteering our time, our actions reflect Christ's compassion for the marginalized and hurting. For instance, organizing community meals for people experiencing homelessness or providing school supplies for underprivileged children showcases our commitment to love our neighbors as ourselves. Giving to causes that align with God's heart—such as missions, education, and social justice—shows the world that our faith is alive and active. This kind of generosity not only meets immediate needs but also points to the character of God, who is generous and loving. Supporting a local charity or contributing to global mission efforts highlights our role in advancing God's Kingdom and positively impacting the world. Matthew 5:16, *"Let your light so shine before men, that they may see your good works, and glorify your Father which is in heaven."* Our good works, including acts of generosity, should be visible to others. Seeing our kindness and generosity prompts them to glorify God and consider the source of our actions—Jesus Christ. Our generous acts can inspire others to seek a relationship with God and cultivate a spirit of giving in their own lives.

Overcoming Obstacles To Generosity

Understanding the barriers that hinder our generosity can help us overcome them and embrace a lifestyle of giving. Many people struggle with the fear that they won't have enough resources to meet their own needs. This fear can prevent us from being generous, as we worry about our necessities—food, clothing, and shelter. Matthew 6:31-33, *"Therefore take no thought, saying, What shall we eat? Or, What shall we drink? Or, Wherewithal shall we be clothed? But seek ye first the kingdom of God, and his righteousness; and all these things shall be added unto you."* God's Kingdom and trust Him to provide for our needs. When we focus on serving Him and others, we can let go of our fears and embrace a lifestyle of generosity. Our culture often emphasizes material wealth and personal accumulation as the keys to happiness. This focus can lead to selfishness, where we prioritize our desires over the needs of others. Luke 12:15, *"And he said unto them, Take heed, and beware of covetousness: for a man's life consisteth not in the abundance of the things which he possesseth."* Recognizing that life is more than just possessions can shift our mindset. True fulfillment comes from serving God and blessing others, not from accumulating wealth for ourselves. The desire to maintain control over our resources can also hinder our generosity. We may feel that if we give, we will lose control over our finances or ability to provide for ourselves and our families. Letting go of control allows God to work in our lives in unexpected and abundant ways.

Cultivating a generous spirit often requires intentional effort to overcome the common obstacles that hinder our giving. Strengthen your trust in God's provision by regularly reminding yourself of His faithfulness. Engage in prayer, study Scripture, and share testimonies of His provision. Acknowledge the times when God has provided for you. This practice will help dispel fears and reinforce your confidence in His ability to meet your needs. Shift your focus from what you lack to what you have. Consider keeping a gratitude journal where you record God's blessings daily or weekly. Recognizing His goodness and the blessings you possess can inspire a more generous heart, making it easier to give to others. If generosity feels overwhelming, begin with small acts of kindness. This could include volunteering your time, sharing your talents, or giving small monetary gifts. Every little act counts, and as you witness the positive impact of your generosity, you may find encouragement to expand your giving. Engage with a community of individuals who practice generosity.

Join groups or ministries that focus on serving others and giving back. Being around generous people can inspire you and provide a supportive environment that encourages a giving mindset. Keep in mind the lasting effects of your generosity. Understand that you are spreading the Gospel and impacting lives eternally by supporting ministries, helping those in need, and contributing to causes aligned with God's heart. Consider how your contributions can lead to changed hearts and lives, reinforcing the importance of your role in God's Kingdom work.

CHAPTER 4

ENTREPRENEURSHIP: CALLING AND PURPOSE IN BUSINESS

Entrepreneurship, the act of creating, managing, and growing a business, is often seen as a purely secular pursuit, but it carries a deeper meaning for the believer. In Scripture, business endeavors are not separate from spiritual life but can be vital to fulfilling one's God-given purpose. Many individuals often separate their work from their spiritual lives, viewing their jobs merely as a means to earn a living. However, the Bible teaches us that our work, including entrepreneurship, is integral to God's divine plan for us. All our actions, including running a business, should be carried out with a heart dedicated to glorifying God. Therefore, entrepreneurship is more than just a path to financial gain or personal achievement; it is a calling that can fulfill God's purposes in the world. The Bible provides numerous examples of individuals who embraced their entrepreneurial talents to advance God's mission. One notable example is Lydia, found in Acts 16:14-15. Lydia was a successful businesswoman specializing in selling purple cloth, a luxury item in her time. After hearing the Apostle Paul preach, Lydia and her household believed and were baptized. She then opened her home to Paul and his companions, offering them hospitality and support for their ministry. Lydia's actions demonstrate how entrepreneurship can be leveraged to support God's work and provide a foundation for ministry. Lydia's business provided for her family and became a platform for spreading the Gospel. Her wealth and position allowed her to influence others and contribute significantly to the early church. This illustrates how entrepreneurship can create opportunities for witnessing and ministry. Lydia's story is a testament to how faith can motivate business practices. She recognized that her success was not solely for her benefit but also to serve others and glorify God. Her willingness to respond to God's calling shows that we can make a lasting impact when we align our business goals with His purpose. Embracing entrepreneurship as a divine calling encourages us to approach our work with purpose and mission. Ensure that your business practices reflect honesty and integrity. Proverbs 11:1 reminds us that the Lord hates dishonest scales, which means we should strive for fairness and transparency in all our dealings. Use your business to serve your community and meet the needs of others.

A foundational principle for entrepreneurs is found in Proverbs 16:3: *"Commit thy works unto the Lord, and thy thoughts shall be established."* Committing our work to God reminds us that He is the ultimate owner of everything we do. We are stewards of the opportunities and resources He provides. This perspective encourages responsible and ethical actions in our business dealings as we recognize that we are accountable to Him. Entrepreneurs are encouraged to seek God's direction in their business decisions through prayer and the study of Scripture. By aligning our plans with His will, we increase the likelihood of success and fulfillment in our efforts. Regularly seeking God's input allows us to make informed decisions that reflect His values.

Another critical principle is Proverbs 11:1, *"A false balance is an abomination to the Lord: but a just weight is his delight."* Conducting business with honesty and fairness is essential. This means being transparent in our dealings, fulfilling our commitments, and respectfully treating customers, employees, and partners. When we operate with integrity, we reflect God's character and build trust within our communities. Short-term gains achieved through dishonest means may lead to immediate success but can ultimately harm our reputation and business. A long-term perspective rooted in integrity helps build a sustainable business that honors God and serves others effectively. Companies should focus on meeting the needs of their customers and communities. When we prioritize serving others, we create a positive impact and establish lasting relationships that can lead to mutual benefit. Consider how your business can contribute to the community and support charitable causes. Generosity helps those in need, reflects the heart of Christ, and can enhance your business's reputation.

Christian entrepreneurs are encouraged to work diligently, making the most of their God-given gifts and talents. This commitment to excellence helps build a successful business and positively impacts the community. When we strive for high standards in our work, we demonstrate integrity and respect for our craft, reflecting God's character in our endeavors. Success often requires perseverance through challenges and setbacks. Diligent entrepreneurs embrace hard work, understanding that it is a pathway to overcoming difficulties and emerging stronger. This perseverance cultivates resilience, enabling them to navigate obstacles and seize new opportunities for growth and advancement. When we exemplify diligence in our work, we can inspire and motivate others to do the same. Our commitment to hard work can encourage employees, partners, and competitors to strive for excellence, creating a culture of diligence in our communities. Our diligent efforts are ultimately for God, and He will reward our labor. By viewing our work as a service to the Lord, we can find motivation and fulfillment in our daily tasks.

Entrepreneurship As A Platform For Ministry

Entrepreneurship presents a unique opportunity for Christians to engage in ministry beyond traditional church settings. Business owners can influence the marketplace, build relationships, and share the love of Christ with those who may never enter a church. This aspect of entrepreneurship highlights the importance of integrating faith into everyday life and work. Matthew 5:16 says, *"Let your light shine before men, that they may see your good works, and glorify your Father which is in heaven."* For Christian entrepreneurs, their businesses can become platforms where their faith shines brightly. By conducting business with excellence, integrity, and generosity, Christian entrepreneurs model the character of Christ. When businesses prioritize ethical practices, treat employees well, and serve customers kindly, they reflect God's love and righteousness. This can attract customers, employees, and competitors to the gospel's message. People are often drawn to businesses that operate on values aligned with Christ, opening doors for conversations about faith. The marketplace provides a unique environment for establishing relationships with diverse individuals. Christian entrepreneurs can create meaningful connections with customers, employees, and suppliers, using these interactions as opportunities to share their faith and the hope found in Christ. Building trust and rapport fosters community, allowing deeper discussions about life and faith. Engaging in community service and supporting local initiatives can further enhance the visibility of a Christian entrepreneur's commitment to Christ. Whether through charitable donations, sponsorships, or volunteer efforts, these acts of service demonstrate a genuine care for others, showcasing the heart of God.

Entrepreneurs can view their businesses as mission fields where they can influence others positively. This perspective encourages them to incorporate biblical principles into their business models, ensuring that their operations reflect God's values. This approach can lead to an environment where employees feel valued and customers feel cared for, all while impacting the community.

By cultivating an environment that encourages open discussions about faith, Christian entrepreneurs can create a workplace where employees feel safe to express their beliefs. This could include starting meetings with prayer, celebrating achievements that align with values, or hosting discussions on faith and work. This atmosphere can help employees grow in their faith and create a sense of unity within the workplace.

Successful entrepreneurs can provide essential funds to support missions, outreach programs, and charitable endeavors. Whether through sponsoring missionary efforts, funding local community outreach, or helping church ministries expand, these financial resources make a tangible difference in spreading the gospel and meeting the needs of the less fortunate. Proverbs 3:9, *"Honour the Lord with thy substance, and with the first fruits of all thine increase."* Christian entrepreneurs are called to give generously from their income, prioritizing God's work by supporting the church, missions, and charitable organizations. Honoring God through tithes, offerings, and unique contributions is an act of worship and trust, recognizing that everything belongs to Him. By using their financial success to invest in kingdom work, entrepreneurs help meet physical and economic needs and contribute to an eternal impact. Their resources can support efforts to spread the gospel, lead people to Christ, and transform lives. Businesses, therefore, become more than profit-generating ventures—they become vessels through which God's purposes can be fulfilled. Christian entrepreneurs can also use their business success to create jobs and empower others. By providing employment, they help individuals and families to thrive, reflecting God's love and care. Empowering others through job creation, mentoring, and equipping them with skills fosters personal and spiritual growth within the community. As entrepreneurs build their businesses and accumulate wealth, they can leave a legacy of generosity for future generations. By instilling in their children and successors the biblical principles of giving and stewardship, they ensure that their resources will continue to be used to honor God and advance

His Kingdom long after they are gone. Entrepreneurship is more than just a means of making a living; it is a powerful platform for ministry by shining its light in the marketplace. The financial resources generated through their businesses can be used to support ministry efforts, further extending their impact on God's kingdom. In embracing this calling, entrepreneurs can fulfill their purpose while making a lasting difference in the lives of others.

Overcoming Challenges In Entrepreneurship

One of the common challenges entrepreneurs face is the temptation to prioritize profits over people, leading to unethical practices and strained relationships. Matthew 6:24 says, *"No man can serve two masters: for either he will hate the one, and love the other, or else he will hold to the one, and despise the other. Ye cannot serve God and mammon."* While profits are essential for a business to survive and grow, Christian entrepreneurs must not allow the pursuit of financial gain to overshadow their responsibility to honor God and care for others. Here are a few ways to navigate this balance: Instead of viewing people merely as customers or employees, prioritize building genuine, respectful relationships. Treat employees fairly, ensure ethical practices with suppliers, and serve customers with integrity and care. By embodying the love of Christ in your interactions, you create an atmosphere of trust and loyalty that strengthens your business over time. While profits are necessary for business success, the mission and purpose of the business should remain at the forefront. Christian entrepreneurs are called to keep their focus on how their work can serve others, create positive change, and advance God's Kingdom. When purpose and service to others drive a business, financial success often follows naturally, but it's no longer the primary goal. Fairness, honesty, and transparency should be central to all business dealings. Making ethical decisions, even when it may result in less profit, reflects trust in God's provision and helps build a business that honors Him. Look for ways the business can positively impact the community, employees, and customers.

Through charitable giving, supporting local causes, or creating job opportunities, entrepreneurs can use their businesses to bless others. This reinforces the idea that success is measured by financial gain and the lasting good the business creates in people's lives.

Entrepreneurship often comes with various pressures, uncertainties, and moments of doubt. During such times, relying solely on personal strength and understanding is easy. However, the Bible calls us to a higher approach. Proverbs 3:5-6, *"Trust in the Lord with all thine heart; and lean not unto thine own understanding. In all thy ways acknowledge him, and he shall direct thy paths."* Instead of relying only on our limited understanding, we are encouraged to seek God's direction and allow Him to lead us through challenging circumstances. In moments of difficulty, make it a habit to pray and meditate on Scripture for wisdom. Whether making critical business decisions or facing challenges, bring your concerns to God. Trust that He will provide clarity and guidance, as He promises to direct our paths when we acknowledge Him in all we do. Surround yourself with fellow believers and entrepreneurs who can offer encouragement, accountability, and wise counsel. Proverbs 15:22, *"Without counsel purposes are disappointed: but in the multitude of counselors they are established."* Being part of a supportive community can make the journey more manageable and allow you to draw strength from others' experiences and insights. Challenges and setbacks are part of the entrepreneurial journey. Rather than becoming discouraged, develop patience and perseverance. Tribulation produces patience, and patience leads to experience and hope. Embrace the process, knowing God uses difficulties to strengthen your character and faith. Reflect on past experiences where God has come through for you. This practice of remembering His faithfulness can give you confidence that He will continue to provide, even in uncertain times. Keeping a journal of God's provisions and answered prayers can be a powerful reminder of His unchanging nature. Trusting in God, seeking support, and staying patient, Christian entrepreneurs can navigate the pressures and uncertainties of business while growing in faith and resilience.

Entrepreneurship And Stewardship

Matthew 25:14-30, *"For the kingdom of heaven is as a man traveling into a far country, who called his servants, and delivered unto them his goods. And unto one he gave five talents, to another two, and another one; to every man according to his several abilities; and straightway took his journey."* In this parable, the master represents God, and the talents symbolize the various gifts, resources, and opportunities He gives us. The expectations set for the servants show that God desires us to use what He has provided actively. The servants who invested and multiplied their talents were praised, while the one who hid his talent out of fear was rebuked. This story offers essential guidance for Christian entrepreneurs, reminding them to use the resources God entrusts to them wisely. Entrepreneurs are called to handle their business finances with care and responsibility. This involves creating sound budgets, saving for the future, investing in areas that promote growth, and maintaining transparency in financial dealings. Proverbs 27:23, *"Be thou diligent to know the state of thy flocks, and look well to thy herds."* This principle encourages entrepreneurs to stay informed and make wise decisions with their finances, ensuring the sustainability of their business while honoring God. Stewardship also includes how entrepreneurs care for their employees. Paying fair wages, creating a healthy work environment, and offering opportunities for personal and professional growth reflect God's justice and compassion. James 5:4 warns against mistreating workers, saying, *"The wages of the laborers...which is of you kept back by fraud, crieth."* Treating employees with respect, fairness, and dignity fosters a positive workplace culture and often leads to increased loyalty and productivity. Christian entrepreneurs are encouraged to use their profits for personal gain and to bless others. This might include supporting charitable causes, funding community initiatives, or contributing to global missions. Acts 20:35 reminds us that "It is more blessed to give than to receive

According to the Bible, stewardship is not about playing it safe but often requires boldness and trust in God to take calculated risks that lead to growth. This principle is clearly illustrated in the Parable of the Talents, where those who took risks by investing were rewarded, while the one who avoided risk out of fear was rebuked. For Christian entrepreneurs, taking risks in faith can lead to opportunities for innovation, expansion, and leaving a meaningful legacy. Entrepreneurs are called to seek growth opportunities that align with God's purposes. This often involves taking steps of faith, whether by innovating with new products, expanding into unfamiliar markets, or adopting new business strategies. Isaiah 43:19 reminds us, "Behold, I will do a new thing; now it shall spring forth; shall ye not know it?" God often opens doors for growth and change but requires faith and trust in His leading. By seeking God's wisdom in these ventures, entrepreneurs can explore opportunities that honor Him while growing their businesses. Christian entrepreneurs have the chance to build a legacy that benefits them in the present and impacts future generations. This legacy can include a commitment to godly business principles, generosity, and community service. Taking risks in faith means trusting God with the opportunities and challenges of entrepreneurship, knowing He will guide and bless endeavors that align with His will.

Entrepreneurship As Part Of God's Purpose For Your Life

God uniquely creates everyone with a specific plan and purpose; for many, that purpose encompasses entrepreneurship. Ephesians 2:10, *"For we are his workmanship, created in Christ Jesus unto good works, which God hath before ordained that we should walk in them."* God has prepared good works for each of us, and for some, these good works involve starting and managing businesses that not only provide for our needs but also reflect God's values and contribute to His Kingdom. As Christian entrepreneurs, we are called to conduct our businesses in a way that mirrors the character of Christ. This means our practices, ethics, and interactions should be infused with integrity, kindness, and love. Doing so fulfills our role as ambassadors for Christ in the marketplace. Our businesses can become platforms for demonstrating the fruits of the Spirit (Galatians 5:22-23, showcasing joy, patience, and goodness to everyone we encounter. Christian entrepreneurship offers a unique platform to fulfill the Great Commission, as described in Matthew 28:19-20. Business owners can integrate their faith into their professional lives, reaching people in ways that extend beyond traditional ministry. Every interaction with customers, clients, employees, and business partners can be an opportunity to demonstrate Christ's love. Entrepreneurs can build genuine relationships that foster trust and respect, creating natural opportunities to share the gospel. Whether through conversations, actions, or creating a welcoming atmosphere, these relationships become practical avenues to show others what it means to follow Jesus. Entrepreneurship can also be a powerful way to support global missions, outreach programs, and ministries financially. As God blesses businesses with success, entrepreneurs can reinvest their profits in causes that spread the gospel, similar to how Lydia, a successful businesswoman in the New Testament, supported Paul and the early church. This allows them to contribute to communities' spiritual growth and well-being locally and worldwide. Christian entrepreneurs can cultivate a workplace that reflects biblical principles and values, encouraging discussions about faith, providing opportunities for prayer, and creating an environment that promotes both professional and spiritual development. By embedding faith into their company's culture, they foster a community where faith can flourish, and employees are encouraged to grow in their relationship with God while thriving in their careers.

Embracing entrepreneurship as part of God's calling for your life is a meaningful journey that requires faith, discernment, and action. Begin by praying for wisdom and clarity in your entrepreneurial journey. James 1:5, *"If any of you lack wisdom, let him ask of God, that giveth to all men liberally, and upbraideth not; and it shall be given him."* Regularly seek God's guidance in your decisions, and be sensitive to the direction He provides through prayer, Scripture, and the counsel of wise, faith-filled individuals. Reflect on how your business can contribute to God's Kingdom. Whether it's through supporting causes you're passionate about or creating products and services that reflect biblical values, allow your work to be a means of furthering God's purpose. By ensuring that your business is in line with God's will, you turn your work into a ministry that blesses others and glorifies God. Entrepreneurship often presents unexpected paths. Be open to where God may lead you, even if it involves stepping outside your comfort zone. Opportunities to serve others, innovate, or expand your business might come in surprising ways. Stay attuned to the needs of your community and industry, and be ready to act on the doors that God opens.

CHAPTER 5

FINANCIAL WISDOM FOR PROSPEROUS LIVING

Money itself is neutral; it can be used for good or ill. Understanding its value means recognizing that it is a tool to fulfill God's work and to support our families and communities. This perspective shifts our focus from accumulating wealth for its own sake to using it wisely to benefit others and honor God. With financial resources comes the responsibility to manage them wisely. Luke 16:10, "He that is faithful in that which is least is faithful also in much." Our ability to handle small amounts of money well reflects our ability to manage more considerable sums responsibly. Being faithful stewards of what we have encourages trustworthiness and integrity. Our financial decisions can have far-reaching effects on our own lives and the lives of those around us. Proverbs 11:25, "The liberal soul shall be made fat: and he that watereth shall be watered also." Generosity and wise giving can create a ripple effect of blessings. When we invest in our communities and help those in need, we foster an environment of support and love. Careful planning and diligence lead to abundance, while rash decisions often result in lack. It encourages us to take the time to create a budget, set financial goals, and think long-term about our financial health. Seeking advice from wise and experienced individuals can provide valuable insights and help us make informed financial decisions. Learning to be content with what we have helps guard against the desire for more, which can lead to poor financial choices and debt. Building solid and supportive relationships can lead to more significant opportunities for financial wisdom. Engaging with others who share similar values can encourage accountability and provide mutual support in financial matters.

Financial wisdom involves understanding the value of money, embracing our responsibilities as stewards, and recognizing the impact of our economic choices. By applying biblical principles, such as diligent planning, seeking counsel, practicing contentment, and investing in relationships, we can manage our resources to honor God and fulfill His purposes. Ultimately, financial wisdom benefits us individually and enables us to bless others and contribute to God's work.

Key Principles Of Financial Wisdom

Budgeting and Planning: Budgeting means creating a plan for how you will spend and save your money each month. It helps you ensure you have enough money for the things you need and keeps you from spending more than you have. Budgeting allows you to save for future goals, emergencies, and investments. When you budget, you tell your money where to go instead of wondering where it went. It gives you control over your finances to meet your needs without unnecessary worry. A budget helps you live within your means, so you don't need credit cards or loans to cover your expenses. With a budget, you can set aside money for emergencies, retirement, and other long-term goals like buying a house or starting a business. Financial stress comes from not knowing how you will pay for your needs. A reasonable budget can reduce that stress by ensuring your money is used wisely. Budgeting allows you to focus on your priorities, whether saving for a car, going on a vacation, or giving generously to others. Start by writing down how much money you earn each month and all your regular expenses, like rent, groceries, utilities, and transportation. This helps you see where your money is going. Make a list of what's most important. Your basic needs, like food, housing, and bills, come first. After that, you can decide how much to save and how much to spend on other things like entertainment or personal expenses. Decide what you want to achieve with your money. This could be paying off debt, saving for a home, or investing for the future. Having clear goals helps you stay focused and motivated. A budget only works if you follow it. Try not to spend more than you've planned; if you do, adjust your spending in other areas to make up for it. Every month, review your budget to see how you're doing. Adjust your budget accordingly if your income changes or you have new expenses. Proverbs 16:3, *"Commit thy works unto the Lord, and thy thoughts shall be established."* Seek God's guidance in all our plans, including managing our finances. When we involve God in our budgeting, we can trust Him to help us make wise decisions. The Bible also teaches that we are stewards of the resources God has given us. Stewardship means managing something that belongs to someone else. In this case, everything we have—including our money—belongs to God, who entrusted us to manage it well. Luke 16:10 says, *"Whoever can be trusted with very little can also be trusted with much."* This means that when we handle our money wisely, God may bless us more. When we budget with God in mind, it's not just about numbers or making more money. It's about honoring God with the resources He's given us. Before creating a budget, pray for wisdom. Ask God to help you make choices that reflect His priorities for your life. He may lead you to save more, give generously, or make sacrifices in certain areas. God calls us to care for the poor and needy (Proverbs 19:17). As you budget, look for ways to include giving in your financial plan. Giving not only blesses others but also brings joy and fulfillment to your life. The Bible warns against the love of money (1 Timothy 6:10) and encourages us to be content with what we have

(Hebrews 13:5). When you budget, remember that having more money or possessions doesn't bring lasting happiness. True contentment comes from trusting God with what we have. Proverbs 6:6-8 talks about the ant, which prepares for the future by storing food during the summer. This teaches us the value of planning and being prepared for future needs. Budgeting allows us to plan for upcoming expenses and be ready for whatever comes our way.

Saving and Investing: Saving means setting aside money for future use. Instead of spending all the money we earn, we put some of it in a safe place, like a bank account, so we can use it when needed. Saving is significant because life can be unpredictable. There might be unexpected situations like medical emergencies, car repairs, or job loss. When we save, we prepare for these challenges so they don't overwhelm us financially. Proverbs 21:20 says, "There is a treasure to be desired and oil in the dwelling of the wise, *but a foolish man spendeth it up.*" A wise person saves their resources, while a foolish person spends everything they have without thinking of the future. Life is full of surprises, and not all of them are good. Saving allows us to have a safety net when things go wrong. When you have money saved, you feel more secure and less stressed because you know you can handle unexpected expenses. Whether buying a house, a car, or paying for your child's education, saving helps you reach big financial goals. Plan on how you will spend your money each month. It enables you to make sure you have enough to save. It adds up even if you can only save a little at a time. It's better to save a small amount regularly than to save nothing. Set up your bank account to automatically transfer money into your savings account every month. This makes saving a habit. Think before you buy. Ask yourself if it's something you need or can live without it.

Investing is using your money to buy something that will grow in value over time. When you invest, you expect to make more money in the future than you have now. Investing is different from saving because it's not just about putting money aside but about making it grow. For example, you can invest in stocks, bonds, or property. These things may increase in value, allowing you to earn more later. While saving is vital for short-term needs and emergencies, investing is essential for long-term goals like retirement or buying a home. Investing involves risk because there's no guarantee of profit, but careful planning can help you build wealth. Investing can help you earn more money than what you put in. Over time, your investments can increase in value and provide additional income. Inflation means that the cost of things goes up over time. If you just save money without investing, your savings may not be worth as much. Investing helps your money keep up with rising costs. If you want to retire comfortably or send your children to college, investing can help you reach those goals. Before you invest, it's essential to understand what you're doing. Learn about different types of investments like stocks, bonds, and real estate. There are many resources online and in books to help you. You don't need a lot of money to start investing. You can begin with small amounts and grow your investment over time. This means spreading your money across different types of investments. If one investment doesn't do well, another might perform better. This helps reduce risk. Investing isn't about getting rich quickly. It requires patience and a long-term mindset. The longer you keep your investments, the more potential they have to grow. Proverbs 21:5, *"The plans of the diligent lead to profit as surely as haste leads to poverty."* This means that careful planning and thoughtful decisions, like saving and investing, lead to success, while quick, careless choices can lead to problems. In the Parable of the Talents (Matthew 25:14-30), Jesus tells the story of a master who gives his servants money (talents) to manage while he is away. Two servants invest the money and make more, while one hides his money and gains nothing. The master praises those who invested wisely but is disappointed with the one who didn't use his money wisely. This parable teaches us that God wants us to be good stewards of what He has given us, which includes managing our finances well. Saving and investing are both essential tools for managing your money wisely. Saving helps you prepare for emergencies and short-term needs, while investing helps your money grow for long-term goals. We honor God with our financial decisions by planning ahead and using what we have wisely.

Avoiding Debt: Debt, especially unnecessary debt, can cause financial stress, limit your ability to save, and hold you back from achieving financial goals. While some debt, like a mortgage or student loans, can be seen as an investment in your future, taking on too much debt or living beyond your means can lead to serious financial difficulties. Being mindful of debt and working to avoid it where possible is a wise strategy for maintaining financial stability and peace of mind. Not all debt is harmful. Some forms of debt, like a mortgage on a home or a loan for education, can be part of a sound financial plan because they can increase your net worth or earning potential. These are considered "good" debts because they are investments that can grow in value over time. On the other hand, "bad" debt, like credit card debt or high-interest loans, often comes from spending on things that don't increase in value. These types of debt can quickly spiral out of control due to high interest rates, making it difficult to pay off and causing financial strain. Romans 13:8, *"Owe no man anything, but to love one another."* The goal is not to owe anyone anything other than love and kindness. The Bible recognizes that debt can lead to feelings of being trapped or enslaved, which can affect our financial health and our emotional and spiritual well-being. Debt can lead to constant worry about how to pay bills or meet financial obligations. This stress can affect your health and relationships. When you borrow money, you often have to pay back more than you borrowed due to interest. The longer it takes to pay off the debt, the more money you lose to interest. If you're tied up with debt payments, it can limit your ability to save, invest, or take advantage of opportunities that could improve your financial future.

It's easy to be tempted by things you want, but if you can't afford it, it's better to wait or save up for it rather than go into debt. Having a budget helps you keep track of your spending and ensures you're not spending money you don't have. A budget also enables you to plan for more considerable expenses to save up instead of borrowing. One of the main reasons people go into debt is because they don't have enough savings to cover unexpected costs, like car repairs or medical bills. Building an emergency fund can help you avoid debt when life throws you a curveball. If you use credit cards, try to pay off the balance in full each month to avoid paying interest. Only charge what you know you can pay off at the end of the month. Write down all your debts, including how much you owe, the interest rates, and the minimum monthly payments. Focus on paying off debts with the highest interest rates first. This will save you money in the long run. If possible, try to pay more than the minimum payment. Even a little extra can help reduce the total amount you owe faster. If you're struggling to get out of debt, don't be afraid to seek help. Financial advisors or credit counseling services can offer guidance and help you create a plan. Proverbs 22:7, *"The rich ruleth over the poor, and the borrower is servant to the lender."* Being in debt can make you feel like you are working for the lender instead of for yourself. The Bible encourages us to avoid becoming enslaved to debt and to strive for financial freedom. Proverbs 22:26-27 advises against taking on debt you can't repay, *"Be not one of them that strike hands, or of them that are sureties for debts. Why should he remove your bed from under thee if thou has nothing to pay?"*

Trusting God with Finances: When we trust Him, it brings peace, confidence, and clarity in how we manage money, helping us to make decisions that align with His will. Philippians 4:19, the Bible tells us, *"But my God shall supply all your need according to his riches in glory by Christ Jesus."* God knows what we need and has the resources to care for us. Trusting God means we can rest in His provision and believe He will care for us according to His perfect plan. One of the first steps in trusting God with finances is seeking His wisdom. Prayer allows God to lead us in making intelligent financial choices. Ask God for guidance in managing your money —creating a budget, saving for the future, or deciding how much to give. Be open to God's direction, knowing He can lead you to make decisions that honor Him and bring peace to your financial life. Gratitude helps us remember how God has provided in the past, strengthening our trust in His future provision. Focusing on what we have instead of what we don't build faith in His ongoing care. Keep a gratitude journal where you write down ways God has blessed you, from daily needs like food and shelter to answered prayers. Reflect on these blessings regularly to remind yourself that God is faithful and will continue to provide.

Trusting God with finances also means trusting Him enough to be generous, even when it feels uncomfortable. Giving, especially in times of financial uncertainty, is a powerful way to show your confidence in God's provision, not just your own resources. Consider giving to your church or those in need, even when your budget is tight, trusting that God will meet your needs. Remember the story of the widow's offering (Mark 12:41-44). Her faith in giving, despite having little, showed a deep trust in God's ability to provide. Jesus reminds us in Matthew 6:25-34 not to worry about our needs, like food and clothing, because God already knows what we need. Instead, we are called to seek God's Kingdom first, trusting that He will handle the rest. When you start to feel anxious about money, take those concerns to God in prayer. Ask Him for peace and to remind you of His faithfulness. Focus on doing what you can, like budgeting and saving, and leave the rest in God's hands. While trusting God, it's also wise to take practical steps in managing money, such as creating an emergency fund. This fund acts as a financial safety net for unexpected expenses, showing responsibility in managing your resources. Set aside a portion of your income each month for an emergency fund. Even small contributions add up over time. This safety net can reduce financial stress, allowing you to focus more on trusting God and less on worrying about the future. Meditating on God's promises about provision strengthens your faith and keeps you grounded in the truth that God will meet your needs. Study and reflect on scriptures that speak of God's faithfulness, like Matthew 7:7-11, which assures us that God desires to give good gifts to His children. Use these verses to remind yourself that God is able and willing to supply your needs.

CHAPTER 6

OVERCOMING CHALLENGES AND TEMPTATIONS OF WEALTH

Wealth, while a blessing from God, can also bring unique challenges and temptations. The Bible is filled with warnings about the dangers of wealth and how it can lead to pride, greed, and a reliance on material possessions rather than God. In this chapter, we will explore these challenges and provide biblical guidance on overcoming the temptations that come with financial success. The goal is to prosper financially and maintain spiritual health and integrity in the face of wealth.

The Danger Of Pride And Self-Sufficiency

As we navigate life, particularly when experiencing financial success or material abundance, a hidden danger emerges: the rise of pride and the temptation of self-sufficiency. When we accumulate wealth, it's easy to forget that God is the trustworthy source of every blessing. Instead of remaining humble, we can drift toward a sense of independence that separates us from God. Deuteronomy 8:17-18, *"And thou say in thine heart, My power and the might of mine hand hath gotten me this wealth. But thou shalt remember the Lord thy God: for it is he that giveth thee power to get wealth."* All our achievements, wealth, and success come from God. It is He who gives us the ability to earn and prosper, and it is essential to remember Him in times of abundance. Forgetting this truth can lead us to believe we are self-sufficient, causing pride to take root in our hearts. Pride and self-sufficiency have dangerous consequences that affect our relationship with God and how we relate to others and live our lives. We can develop a sense of superiority when we believe our achievements are solely the result of our hard work and talent. This attitude leads to looking down on others who may not be as financially successful. It distances us from the humility that God desires in us. It causes us to forget that everything we have is a gift from God. It weakens our empathy and willingness to help others, central to Christian love and service.

Pride can cause us to become spiritually blind. When we feel like we have everything under control, we may lose sight of our deep need for God. This self-sufficiency can lead to a lack of prayer and spiritual discipline. It creates a false sense of independence, where we no longer rely on God. We may become disconnected from God, believing we can handle everything ourselves. It can hinder spiritual growth, as we no longer seek God's wisdom or guidance. Pride can also lead to isolation. We might pull away from others when we focus too much on maintaining our status, wealth, or possessions. Instead of reaching out to help those in need, we become concerned with protecting our resources and success. It leads to a lack of generosity and compassion, which God calls us to live out. Isolation from others can cause us to miss out on the blessing of community and the opportunity to grow through serving others. It may create loneliness, as pride keeps us from forming genuine connections. The danger of pride and self-sufficiency is that it pulls us away from God and the life He desires. Wealth and success are not inherently wrong, but when they cause us to forget our dependence on God, we fall into spiritual danger. The Bible reminds us to stay humble, acknowledge that all our blessings come from God, and resist the temptation to believe we are self-sufficient.

Overcoming Pride And Self-Sufficiency

Pride and self-sufficiency can sneak into our lives, especially when we experience success or accumulate wealth. To stay humble and reliant on God, it's essential to cultivate habits and attitudes that actively keep pride in check. Humility recognizes that every blessing and success comes from God, not our efforts alone. Regularly remind yourself of God's goodness and your reliance on Him. *"Humble yourselves in the sight of the Lord, and he shall lift you."* James 4:10. By humbling ourselves before God, we allow Him to elevate us in His time, according to His will. Gratitude helps us remember that all we have is a gift from God. By thanking God for the blessings in our lives, we counteract pride and reinforce our reliance on Him. Start a gratitude journal where you can list things you're thankful for daily, focusing on how God has provided for you. A heart filled with gratitude is less likely to fall into the trap of pride.

Generosity is a powerful way to remind ourselves that we are stewards of what God has given us. When we share with others, we actively demonstrate our trust in God, not our wealth or possessions. *"Charge them that are rich in this world, that they are not highminded, nor trust in uncertain riches, but in the living God, who giveth us richly all things to enjoy."* 1 Timothy 6:17-18. Sharing with others reinforces our understanding that everything we have belongs to God, and we are called to use it for His purposes. God's Word provides constant reminders of our need for Him and keeps us grounded in truth. Regular reading and meditation on Scripture helps us stay humble and aware of our dependence on God. *"When pride cometh, then cometh shame: but with the lowly is wisdom."* Proverbs 11:2. The Bible teaches wisdom is found in humility, while pride leads to downfall. Staying connected to the

Word helps guard against pride. A community of believers who can encourage you, provide guidance, and hold you accountable is crucial in maintaining humility. Accountability helps us stay focused on God and avoid the isolation that pride can cause. Overcoming pride and self-sufficiency requires intentional effort, but by practicing humility, cultivating gratitude, sharing generously, staying connected to God's Word, and seeking accountability, we can live lives that are pleasing to God. When we keep our hearts humble and our trust firmly in the Lord, we can experience the fullness of His blessings without falling into the traps of pride.

The Temptation Of Greed And Materialism

Greed is a powerful temptation that often accompanies pursuing wealth and material success. It creates an insatiable desire for more money, possessions, and recognition—yet it never truly satisfies the soul. As believers, it's crucial to guard our hearts against the pull of greed and materialism. Jesus warns us directly about this danger in Luke 12:15. *"Take heed, and beware of covetousness: for a man's life consisteth not in the abundance of the things which he possesseth."* Life's value is not material wealth but our relationship with God and how we live out His purpose. The Bible also identifies the love of money as the root of all evil. 1 Timothy 6:10, *"For the love of money is the root of all evil: which while some coveted after, they have erred from the faith, and pierced themselves through with many sorrows."* It's not money itself that is harmful, but the obsession with it that can lead us away from God and into sorrow. Greed fuels this unhealthy pursuit and distracts us from a Christ-centered life.

To combat the temptation of greed, we must cultivate contentment and trust in God's provision. Paul sets a powerful example of contentment in Philippians 4:11-12. *"Not that I speak in respect of want: for I have learned, in whatsoever state I am, in addition to that, to be content. I know both how to be abased, and I know how to abound."* Paul learned to find peace and satisfaction in every situation, whether in abundance or need. This contentment comes from trusting that God will provide what we truly need. Instead of pursuing temporary wealth, Jesus urges us to store treasures in heaven. By investing in eternal things—such as relationships, serving others, and spiritual growth—we align our hearts with God's purposes. Generosity is one of the best antidotes to greed. When we give freely, we shift from accumulating more for ourselves to blessing others. 2 Corinthians 9:6-7 encourages us to give cheerfully, knowing that God loves a generous giver. Overcoming the temptations of greed and materialism requires a heart rooted in contentment and trust in God's provision. Wealth and material possessions are fleeting, but a life dedicated to God brings lasting fulfillment and joy. As we focus on eternal riches and seek to live generously, we free ourselves from the chains of greed and live out God's purpose.

The Deception Of Security In Wealth

Wealth can create a false sense of security, making us feel safe and self-sufficient. This subtle but dangerous shift can lead us to trust our financial resources rather than God, misplacing our reliance on the actual provider of everything. While financial stability is essential, it's crucial to recognize the fleeting nature of earthly riches. Proverbs 18:11, *"The rich man's wealth is his strong city and as a high wall in his conceit."* We may think our financial resources will protect us from life's uncertainties, but this mindset is deceptive. In Luke 12:16-21, Jesus tells the parable of the rich fool. Here, a wealthy man accumulates great riches and stores them all for himself, believing he has secured his future. However, that very night, his life is taken from him, rendering his wealth useless. Jesus concludes the parable with a warning: *"So is he that layeth up treasure for himself, and is not rich toward God."* Our earthly wealth can vanish instantly, and proper security lies in our relationship with God, not material possessions. To combat the deception of security in wealth, we must anchor our trust in God rather than material possessions. While others may rely on their wealth or resources, our proper security comes from trusting God's unchanging and eternal nature. Instead of focusing solely on accumulating wealth, we should invest in things with infinite value. We build a secure foundation beyond this life by prioritizing our relationship with God and serving others. Generosity can help break the hold of materialism. When we give to others, we acknowledge that our wealth is a blessing meant to be. Sharing what we have not only blesses others but also helps us maintain a proper perspective on our resources.

The Challenge Of Maintaining Generosity

One of the paradoxes of wealth is that the more we accumulate, the harder it can become to give. As our financial resources grow, the temptation to hoard them can increase, driven by fear of losing what we have or not having enough for the future. This mindset contradicts the biblical principle of generosity, which encourages us to share and bless others. When we give, we are not losing but sowing into something more significant. We open ourselves to receiving even more from God by sharing what we have. The challenge lies in ensuring our wealth serves eternal purposes rather than temporary gains. Our hearts follow our investments, so prioritizing heavenly treasures shifts our focus from accumulating earthly wealth to contributing to God's work. Remember how God has generously provided for us. Reflecting on His blessings can inspire us to share with others, acknowledging that everything we have is His gift. Establish a regular percentage of your income to give away. Making generosity a priority rather than an afterthought helps cultivate a habit of giving. Whether it's 10% or another amount, setting a goal ensures we remain intentional about our generosity. Actively seek ways to bless others through your church, local charities, or individual acts of kindness. Being aware of the needs around us allows us to respond generously when we can, turning our blessings into blessings for others. Ask God to help you cultivate a spirit of generosity and overcome fears holding you back from giving. Prayer opens our hearts to His guidance, allowing us to see opportunities to share and bless others more clearly.

Navigating The Temptation Of Compromise

With wealth often comes influence and opportunity. While these can be used for good, they tempt us to compromise our values for more significant financial gain or success. This can lead to unethical business practices, dishonesty, or a willingness to do whatever it takes to increase profit. It's essential to navigate these temptations with wisdom and integrity. In Matthew 6:24, *"No man can serve two masters: for either he will hate the one, and love the other, or else he will hold to the one, and despise the other. Ye cannot serve God and mammon."* The pull to compromise often arises when we try to serve God and money. Jesus clarifies that this is impossible; we must choose whom we will serve. We risk losing our integrity and purpose when we prioritize wealth above our faith. Proverbs 16:8 also reminds us of the value of integrity. *"Better is a little with righteousness than great revenues without right."*

Even if it means earning less, upholding righteousness and godly principles holds far more value in God's eyes than compromising for wealth. Choosing integrity over greed fosters a closer relationship with God and honors Him. To navigate the temptation of compromise, define your core values and let them guide your financial decisions. Writing them down and revisiting them regularly helps ensure alignment with your actions. Knowing what you stand for strengthens your resolve against temptation. Surround yourself with trusted friends or mentors who can hold you accountable in your business practices and decisions. Having a support system encourages transparency and reinforces your commitment to integrity. Commit to honesty in all your financial dealings, even when challenging. Being transparent builds trust and honors God. It also establishes a solid foundation for relationships in business and personal life.

Regularly seek God's wisdom in your financial decisions. Ask Him to help you prioritize righteousness over profit. Prayer opens our hearts to His guidance, helping us make choices that reflect our values. Before pursuing a financial opportunity, assess whether it aligns with your values and whether it requires compromising your integrity. Taking time to evaluate ensures you make decisions that honor God and maintain your moral compass.

Avoiding The Isolation That Can Come With Wealth

One of the subtle challenges of wealth is the isolation it can create. As wealth increases, there can be a tendency to withdraw from others, driven by fear of being taken advantage of or a desire to protect what we have. Additionally, wealth can lead to loneliness as relationships become strained by financial disparities. Wealth can sometimes create barriers that lead to isolation. To avoid this loneliness and foster meaningful relationships. Make a conscious effort to maintain relationships with friends and family, regardless of your financial situation. Schedule regular gatherings, phone calls, or video chats to nurture these connections. Staying in touch helps remind you that relationships are more valuable than material wealth. Look for opportunities to share your resources with others. This could include acts of kindness, charitable giving, or supporting those in need. Sharing can foster connection and community, showing that your wealth is not just for personal gain but also uplifting others. Get involved in local events or groups that interest you, such as volunteering, sports, or hobby clubs. Participating in these activities can help you meet new people and build meaningful relationships. Engaging with your community allows you to connect with others who share your interests and values. Approach relationships with a spirit of humility. Remember that wealth does not define your worth or value as a person. Treat everyone with respect and kindness, regardless of their financial status. Humility opens the door to genuine connections and helps you appreciate the diverse experiences of others. Use your wealth and knowledge to mentor others. This helps those in need, fosters deeper connections, and combats feelings of isolation. Mentoring allows you to share your journey and wisdom, creating bonds with those you support and enriching your life and theirs.

CHAPTER 7

WEALTH AS A TOOL FOR MINISTRY AND OUTREACH

Wealth is not merely a means of personal enjoyment or comfort when understood from a biblical perspective. It is a powerful ministry and outreach tool designed to extend the love, grace, and message of the Kingdom of God. This chapter will explore how wealth can be used effectively to impact lives, advance God's work on earth, and bring hope and salvation to those in need. Through both the Old and New Testament scriptures, we see examples of how God's people were blessed financially so they could be a blessing to others. When correctly managed, wealth becomes a resource that opens doors to serve, evangelize, and uplift those around us. We will explore practical ways believers can use their wealth for ministry, discuss the biblical foundation for giving, and highlight the eternal rewards from faithful stewardship of financial resources.

Wealth As A Blessing To Others

The Bible teaches that one of the primary reasons God blesses His people with wealth is so they can be a blessing to others. Understanding this principle helps us see wealth not merely as personal gain but as a tool for serving and uplifting those around us. Genesis 12:2-3 *"I will make of thee a great nation, and I will bless thee, and make thy name great, and thou shalt be a blessing."* This promise illustrates that God's blessings, including wealth, are intended to flow outward to benefit others. Wealth is part of God's plan to enable us to bless those in need. Proverbs 19:17 further emphasizes this principle: *"He that hath pity upon the poor lendeth unto the Lord; and that which he hath given will he pay him again."* When we use our wealth to help the needy, we align ourselves with God's mission to care for the least among us. Generosity is not just a good deed; it's a partnership with God's work. The church has historically relied on the generosity of believers to carry out its mission. In the early church, Acts 4:34-35, *"Neither was there any among them that lacked: for as many as were possessors of lands or houses sold them, and brought the prices of the things that were sold, and laid them down at the apostles' feet: and distribution was made unto every man according as he had need."* The early believers understood that their wealth was a resource meant to care for the community and advance the Gospel.

Identify needs within your community or church and contribute financially or through service. Whether supporting a local charity or helping a needy family, every act of generosity matters. Use your skills and connections to help others. Sometimes, your knowledge or network can be just as valuable as financial assistance. Sharing your expertise can empower others to improve their situations. Share your giving experiences with friends and family to inspire them to contribute to causes they care about. Discussing the impact of your generosity can motivate others to take action. Regularly seek God's direction on how to use your wealth for His purposes. Ask for wisdom to discern where your contributions will make the most impact, trusting that God will lead you to those in need.

Using Wealth To Spread The Gospel

Wealth offers unique opportunities to further the mission of spreading the Gospel. Financial resources are crucial in evangelism, discipleship, and outreach, empowering believers to share the message of Jesus both locally and globally. One biblical example of this is the Apostle Paul, whose ministry was sustained by the generosity of believers. Philippians 4:16-1, Paul acknowledges the support he received: *"For even in Thessalonica ye sent once and again unto my necessity. Not because I desire a gift, but fruit that may abound to your account."* Paul's gratitude was not rooted in personal gain but in the spiritual rewards resulting from their giving. The Philippian church's contributions enabled him to focus on his mission of spreading the Gospel, showing that financial support is an investment in God's Kingdom with eternal benefits. Today, believers can follow the example of the early church by using their wealth to advance God's work in various ways. Many missionaries rely on financial support to sustain their work in challenging environments. Contributing to their needs, you help them focus on sharing the Gospel without financial distractions. Establishing new churches requires significant resources. By investing in church planting initiatives, you help create new communities of faith where people can hear the message of Jesus. Distributing Bibles and Christian resources is essential for equipping believers. Your financial contributions can make these materials accessible to those who might otherwise not have access. With the rise of technology, media ministries can reach millions worldwide. By supporting these efforts, you help amplify the message of Jesus through television, radio, social media, and other platforms. Local ministries often need financial resources to fund food programs, community services, and events designed to share the Gospel. Your wealth can help meet the physical and spiritual needs of your community. Wealth is a powerful tool that, when used for God's purposes, can have a lasting impact on the spread of the Gospel. As believers, we are called to use our resources to further the work of Christ, ensuring that His message reaches those near and far. We partner in God's mission through giving and investing in something that yields eternal rewards.

Meeting Practical Needs Through Financial Blessings

One of the most potent ways wealth can be used is to address the practical needs of individuals and communities. Financial blessings offer tangible resources like food, shelter, healthcare, and education. By doing so, we can demonstrate the love of Christ in real and impactful ways. The Bible emphasizes the importance of meeting the practical needs of others. James 2:15-16, *"If a brother or sister be naked, and destitute of daily food, and one of you say unto them, Depart in peace, be ye warmed and filled; notwithstanding ye give them, not those things which are needful to the body; what doth it profit?"* Words alone are insufficient if we fail to take action to help those who are struggling. Similarly, Proverbs 3:27 urges us, *"Withhold not good from them to whom it is due, when it is in the power of thine hand to do it."* When we can help, God calls us to use our resources to bless others. Donating funds or resources to food banks, shelters, and relief organizations is a practical way to meet the essential needs of people in crisis. Your contributions can help ensure that no one goes without necessities like food and shelter. Supporting healthcare initiatives, clinics, or organizations that provide medical services to underprivileged communities can significantly improve lives. This might include funding health clinics, providing medical supplies, or supporting health education programs. Education is a vital area where financial blessings can make a lasting impact. Scholarships, school supplies, and funding for educational programs can empower individuals to break the cycle of poverty and create opportunities for personal growth and community development. Christians in business can help meet financial needs by creating jobs and offering fair wages. This provides economic stability for individuals and their families and fosters dignity, self-sufficiency, and hope for the future. Funding community development projects, such as building infrastructure, supporting local businesses, or enhancing access to services, can lead to long-term improvements in living conditions and help lift entire communities out of poverty. Efforts to meet practical needs often create opportunities for deeper conversations about faith and the love of God. When we demonstrate Christ's love through actions, we build trust and relationships with those we serve. This trust can lead to openings to share the Gospel and show how God not only meets physical needs but also addresses spiritual ones. As we provide practical help, we reflect the heart of Jesus, who cared for the physical and spiritual well-being of those He encountered. Using wealth to meet practical needs is one of the most meaningful ways to show others God's love. By addressing the physical needs of those around us, we open doors for deeper relationships and opportunities to share the Gospel. Wealth is not just for personal gain; it is a tool God gives to bless others and advance His Kingdom on Earth.

The Eternal Rewards Of Kingdom Investment

Investing our wealth in God's Kingdom goes beyond meeting immediate needs; it has eternal significance. The Bible teaches that our financial decisions can yield spiritual dividends that last forever, encouraging us to prioritize heavenly treasures over earthly wealth. In Matthew 6:19-20, *"Lay not up for yourselves treasures upon earth, where moth and rust doth corrupt, and where thieves break through and steal: But lay up for yourselves treasures in heaven."* While earthly treasures can be lost or destroyed, the impact of our generosity and service for God's Kingdom remains eternally secure. Every act of generosity, no matter how small, plays a vital role in God's Kingdom. Jesus teaches us in Matthew 10:4, *"And whosoever shall give to drink unto one of these little ones a cup of cold water only in the name of a disciple, verily I say unto you, he shall in no wise lose his reward."* No act of kindness goes unnoticed by God. Even the simplest gesture, when done with love and a pure heart, has significant and lasting effects in the spiritual realm. When we give compassionately, we plant seeds that will grow and bear fruit for eternity. Every act of kindness, every gift, whether it's our time, resources, or encouragement, helps advance God's Kingdom. These seeds of generosity may not always produce immediate results, but they influence lives and lead others to Christ. God values the size of the gift and the sincerity with which it is given. As we contribute to the needs of others, whether through small daily acts or more considerable sacrifices, we are part of God's eternal plan, showing His love and grace to the world.

When we use our wealth to support ministries and help those in need, we plant seeds that can bring about eternal transformation. Our financial blessings become instruments in God's hands, used to touch lives and build His Kingdom. By funding missionaries and evangelistic efforts, we help spread the Gospel to places we may never visit. Our contributions lead souls to Christ, expanding God's Kingdom and bringing hope to unreached communities. Meeting the practical needs of others— such as providing food, shelter, medical care, and education— demonstrates Christ's love in action. These acts of generosity can open doors to sharing the Gospel, showing that God cares for their physical and spiritual well-being. Contributing to programs that disciple new believers ensures they are nurtured in their faith. This helps them grow spiritually, equipping them to share the Gospel and invest in the lives of others, multiplying the impact of our giving. Supporting local churches and community initiatives helps create solid and faith-centered communities. These communities foster spiritual growth, provide fellowship, and ensure that more people encounter the life-changing message of Christ. The Bible teaches that God promises eternal rewards for those who faithfully steward their resources for His Kingdom. This assurance motivates us to give generously and serve others joyfully, knowing that our efforts have lasting significance. As we invest in God's work—whether through supporting ministries, helping the needy, or spreading the Gospel—we honor Him and contribute to something far more significant than ourselves. Jesus reminds us of this eternal promise in Matthew 6:20: "But store up for yourselves treasures in heaven, where neither moth nor rust destroys, and where thieves do not break in or steal." Our contributions will bear fruit for eternity, leading to everlasting joy and fulfillment in His presence. This truth encourages us to focus on eternal rewards rather than temporary gains, trusting that God sees and rewards every faithful act. Using our wealth to advance God's Kingdom is a profound way to invest in eternity. We can make a lasting impact that echoes through the ages by prioritizing heavenly treasures and remaining faithful in our generosity. Let us embrace the privilege of partnering with God in His work, knowing that every act of kindness and every investment made for His glory will yield eternal rewards.

CHAPTER 8

LEAVING A LEGACY: WEALTH FOR FUTURE GENERATIONS

L eaving a legacy is more than just financial inheritance; it's about passing down values, faith, and a God-centered vision to guide future generations. When aligned with God's purposes, wealth can be a significant part of this legacy. This chapter will explore how believers can leave a lasting impact on their children, families, and communities by using wealth for spiritual and material blessing, ensuring that it continues to serve God's Kingdom for years. The concept of inheritance in the Bible goes beyond mere financial assets; it encompasses the spiritual, moral, and ethical legacies we leave for future generations. Understanding the importance of inheritance ensures that our legacy reflects God's values and purposes. Proverbs 13:22 says, "A good man leaveth an inheritance to his children's children: and the sinner's wealth is laid up for the just." A sound financial inheritance can help alleviate burdens and create opportunities for our children and grandchildren to thrive. It's essential to plan for the future by saving and investing wisely. This includes making financial decisions that align with biblical principles, such as avoiding debt and living within our means. We should teach our children and grandchildren about wise financial management as we build wealth. This education will empower them to handle the resources entrusted to them responsibly. While financial resources are significant, the most crucial inheritance we can leave is one of faith and spiritual guidance. This involves living out our faith authentically, which sets a powerful example for future generations. As they witness our relationship with God, they are more likely to embrace that faith for themselves. Sharing the lessons we've learned throughout our walk with God—successes and failures—can provide invaluable insight for our children and grandchildren. This wisdom can guide them in their spiritual journeys. Teaching our children the importance of integrity, compassion, and service reflects our commitment to God's Word. By emphasizing these values, we help them understand the significance of living according to biblical principles. Encouraging regular prayer, Bible study, and involvement in church and community fosters a vibrant faith that can be passed down through generations. As believers, it is essential to recognize that material wealth should serve God's purposes. When we leave an inheritance, it should be accompanied by teachings on using those resources wisely and in alignment with God's will. Teaching our heirs the importance of generosity ensures that the wealth they inherit will be used to bless others, continuing the cycle of giving and serving. Encouraging our children to use their financial resources to support ministry, missions, and charitable work reinforces the idea that wealth is a tool for God's work, not just personal gain.

Passing Down Biblical Principles Of Stewardship

Teaching future generations about stewardship is one of the most valuable legacies you can offer. Stewardship is not just about managing wealth; it's about honoring God with the resources He has entrusted us. By instilling biblical stewardship principles in our children and grandchildren, we prepare them for a life of faithfulness and responsibility. Proverbs 22:6 *"Train up a child in the way he should go: and when he is old, he will not depart from it.''* This emphasizes that teaching stewardship from a young age is essential in shaping lifelong habits and values. When children are taught about God's stewardship principles, they are better equipped to make wise financial decisions in the future. Begin by instilling the biblical truth that God owns everything, and we are simply caretakers of His blessings (Psalm 24:1). Teach children that their financial resources are tools to serve God and others, not just for personal gain. Encourage them to develop a mindset of generosity, responsibility, and gratitude. Practical application is critical to reinforcing these teachings. Help your children set austere budgets, save for specific goals, and practice giving. Involving them in family discussions about financial decisions helps them see stewardship in action, fostering a deeper understanding of managing resources that honor God.

Teach your children the joy of giving. Show them how to be generous, not just with their money but also their time and talents. This can include donating to those in need, supporting church activities, or volunteering in the community. Help them understand the importance of making wise investments. This could involve educating them about saving for the future, understanding the value of compound interest, and making informed spending decisions. Teach them the dangers of debt and the importance of living within their means. Discuss the implications of borrowing and how to make wise choices regarding loans and credit.

Accountability to God. Instill in them the understanding that they are accountable to God for managing their resources. This can encourage them to seek God's guidance in their financial decisions through prayer and Scripture. Children learn more from observing their parents and grandparents than what they are told. By modeling responsible stewardship in your own life, you provide a living example for them to follow. Share your financial decisions with your children, explaining the reasoning behind them. This transparency can foster trust and open discussions about stewardship. Show your children how you trust God in your financial matters. Share stories of how God has provided for you and how you have seen His faithfulness in your life. Encourage family traditions focusing on giving and stewardship, such as a family charity fund or a yearly service project. These experiences can practically instill the importance of stewardship. Passing biblical stewardship principles is a profound gift that equips future generations to honor God with their resources. By teaching them about generosity, wise investing, avoiding debt, and accountability to God, you are setting them up for a lifetime of faithful stewardship. As you model these principles in your own life, you create a lasting culture of stewardship that will impact your family for years to come.

Building A Family Legacy Of Generosity

Generosity is more than just a financial practice; it's a mindset that can shape the values and character of future generations. By instilling a legacy of generosity, we help our children and grandchildren view wealth as a means to bless others and advance God's Kingdom. This understanding transforms their approach to wealth and enriches their lives profoundly. Acts 20:35, *"It is more blessed to give than to receive."* Teaching future generations this principle can lead to a life marked by gratitude and a desire to serve others. Help your family see that wealth is a resource for doing good. Emphasize that the accurate measure of wealth is not what we accumulate but how we use it to bless others. Teaching generosity equips children with essential life skills like empathy, kindness, and a sense of responsibility. These traits are crucial for their personal development and their interactions with others. Establish regular family gatherings focused on giving. Use these times to discuss needs in the community or around the world and decide together how your family can respond. This not only creates a shared mission but also builds unity. Involve your children in charitable activities. This could include volunteering at a local shelter, participating in community cleanups, or organizing fundraisers for a cause your family cares about. Hands-on experiences teach the value of giving in a practical way. Encourage your family to support church missions and outreach programs. Whether through financial contributions or service projects, involvement in these efforts reinforces the importance of serving others in the name of Christ.

Create a family budget that includes a specific allocation for charitable giving. Discuss and choose the causes that resonate with your family values, ensuring everyone is involved in decision-making. Celebrate milestones or holidays with acts of giving. For example, consider donating to a charity in each other's name instead of exchanging gifts on birthdays. This reinforces the idea that giving is a reason for celebration. Consider establishing a family foundation or charitable trust. This allows your family to make long-term contributions to causes aligned with your values, ensuring that your legacy of generosity continues even after you are gone. By embedding the value of generosity into the fabric of your family's identity, you create a legacy that extends beyond financial resources. Generosity nurtures a deeper relationship with God. As your family experiences the blessings of giving, they will learn to trust God's provision and recognize the joy of serving others. A legacy of generosity can inspire others within your community. Your family's commitment to giving can encourage friends, neighbors, and future generations to adopt similar practices, creating a ripple effect of kindness and compassion. Building a family legacy of generosity is a powerful way to influence the hearts and minds of future generations. By teaching them to view wealth as a tool for blessing others and actively involving them in charitable efforts, you help cultivate a spirit of generosity that lasts a lifetime. Together, you can create a lasting impact on your family, community, and the world, demonstrating the love of Christ through your actions.

Wealth For The Glory Of God, Not Personal Gain

When discussing wealth within a family, it is vital to clarify that the ultimate aim is not personal gain but rather the glory of God. Leaving a legacy of wealth can be a powerful tool for advancing God's Kingdom when approached with the right mindset. Ecclesiastes 5:10 warns us: *"He that loveth silver shall not be satisfied with silver; nor he that loveth abundance with increase: this is also vanity."* It reminds us that the quest for riches can lead to dissatisfaction and emptiness. Instead, true fulfillment comes from using wealth to serve God and others. Help your family understand that wealth should be a tool for achieving greater purposes. Rather than seeking wealth for status or comfort, it should be directed toward fulfilling God's will on earth. Encourage discussions around how wealth can be utilized to support ministries, charitable organizations, and missions that spread the Gospel. This focus shifts the narrative from personal accumulation to collective impact for the glory of God. Demonstrate through your actions how to use wealth to bless others. Share stories of how your financial decisions have advanced God's work or met the needs of others, illustrating the joy that comes from generosity. As a family, discuss your values surrounding money. Encourage open conversations about using your resources for God's glory. This sets a foundation that future generations can build upon. Develop family guidelines for how to handle inherited wealth. This might include commitments to give a certain percentage to charity, invest in community projects, or support local churches. These guidelines serve as a framework for making decisions that honor God.

Equipping your family to use their inheritance wisely, you are helping them ensure that their wealth carries eternal significance. Teach your children that actual investments lie in the lives they touch and the Kingdom work they support. Encourage them to look for opportunities where their resources can create lasting change, whether through education, healthcare, or spiritual outreach. Help future generations recognize that while earthly rewards may be fleeting, the impact of their generosity can have eternal consequences. They can find comfort in Matthew 6:20: "But lay up for yourselves treasures in heaven, where neither moth nor rust doth corrupt, and where thieves do not break through nor steal." In leaving a legacy of wealth, it is essential to understand that wealth should be used for God's glory rather than personal gain. By emphasizing the purpose of wealth to advance God's Kingdom, future generations will be equipped to use their resources to honor God, serve others, and contribute to eternal significance. This approach ensures that the legacy of wealth becomes a powerful testament to God's provision and love, impacting lives now and for future generations.

Creating A Plan For Generational Impact

Start by assessing your current financial situation. Create a detailed budget for your assets, liabilities, and future financial goals. This foundational work helps ensure that your resources can be used effectively for both immediate needs and long-term objectives. A will is essential for outlining how your assets should be distributed after passing. It ensures that your wishes are honored and can prevent disputes among heirs. Trusts can provide greater control over how your wealth is distributed, allowing you to designate specific uses for your assets, such as funding education or charitable giving. If you have minor children, appoint guardians to care for them in your absence. This decision reflects your values and ensures your children are raised in an environment that aligns with your beliefs. Integrate your faith into your planning process. This might include consulting with spiritual leaders or mentors who can provide biblical insights and encourage you to reflect on how your wealth can serve God's purposes.

Consider composing a letter to your heirs that outlines your hopes and aspirations for how they will use their inheritance. Include Your faith journey and how it shaped your approach to wealth. Biblical principles that guided your life and financial decisions.

Encouragement for them to continue pursuing a life that honors God. Work with your family to develop a mission statement that expresses your collective commitment to using wealth for Kingdom purposes. This statement should reflect core values and aspirations. Regularly review it to ensure that all financial decisions align with this vision. Establish a routine for family discussions about finances and legacy planning. These meetings create an opportunity to share updates, review goals, and address any changes in circumstances. Engage your children and grandchildren in financial discussions from an early age. Teach them about budgeting, saving, and giving. This involvement helps them appreciate the value of stewardship and prepares them to manage wealth responsibly. Periodically assess how well your family is adhering to the legacy plan. Are they actively engaging in charitable giving? Are they making financial decisions that reflect your shared mission statement? Adjustments may be necessary to keep the vision alive. Creating a plan for generational impact requires diligence, foresight, and a commitment to aligning wealth with God's purposes. By developing a comprehensive strategy that includes financial planning, legal considerations, and spiritual guidance, you can ensure that your legacy continues to impact generations to come positively. By effectively communicating your vision and values, you empower your heirs to honor your legacy and further the work of God's Kingdom. This intentional approach cultivates a lasting inheritance reflecting financial wisdom and a deep commitment to faith.

Avoiding The Pitfalls Of Wealth In Future Generations

Wealth can be a double-edged sword. While it has the potential to bless families and advance God's Kingdom, it can also lead to challenges for future generations who may not have faced the same hardships or learned valuable lessons from their predecessors. Ecclesiastes 7:11-12 reminds us: *"Wisdom is good with an inheritance: and by it there is profit to them that see the sun.*

For wisdom is a defense, and money is a defense: but the excellency of knowledge is that wisdom giveth life to them that have it." Without a solid understanding of stewardship, heirs may not appreciate the value of money and could squander their inheritance on unnecessary or frivolous expenses. Lack of financial literacy can lead to poor investment decisions, resulting in loss rather than growth of the family's wealth. Wealth can create a sense of entitlement, where heirs may feel they deserve luxury without understanding the work and sacrifice that generated the wealth. Inheritance disputes can arise among family members, leading to division and conflict. Wealth can become a source of greed and bitterness if not adequately managed.

Start by fostering a culture of discipleship within the family. Teach children and grandchildren the importance of faith, hard work, and the biblical principles that guide financial stewardship. Regular family devotions can help instill these values. Encourage your heirs to connect with mentors who embody wise financial stewardship and have a strong faith. These relationships can provide guidance and support as they learn to manage wealth responsibly. Ensure that future generations have a solid understanding of biblical teachings on money. This includes principles of generosity, the dangers of greed, and the importance of using wealth for God's purposes. Provide opportunities for financial education. This can consist of Workshops or courses on budgeting, investing, and wealth management. Resources such as books, seminars, or online courses that emphasize stewardship from a biblical perspective. Establish systems of accountability to help heirs manage their wealth responsibly. This can involve Regular financial reviews and discussions to assess how resources are being used. Setting up joint accounts for charitable giving or investment to encourage collective decision-making.

As a parent or grandparent, demonstrate wise financial practices in your own life. Share your financial journey, including successes and failures, to provide real-life lessons. Involve your family in charitable giving and service projects. Helping those in need fosters a spirit of generosity and counters entitlement. Develop a plan that outlines how wealth should be used and its associated values. This plan should be revisited regularly and can include specific instructions on charitable giving or investment strategies that align with your family's mission. Encourage regular prayer and reflection on how to use wealth wisely. Seeking God's guidance in financial matters helps align decisions with His will and fosters a spirit of humility and gratitude. Avoiding the pitfalls of wealth in future generations requires intentionality, wisdom, and spiritual maturity. Equipping heirs with the knowledge and understanding necessary to handle wealth can help safeguard your family's legacy from being mismanaged or squandered. Through intentional discipleship, financial education, and accountability, future generations will be better prepared to honor God with their inheritance, turning potential challenges into opportunities for growth and service. In doing so, they can continue the legacy of faith, stewardship, and generosity you have established.

Investing In What Truly Matters

In our journey through life, the legacies we leave behind are often measured by the material wealth we accumulate. However, Jesus calls us to adopt an eternal perspective on legacy. Material wealth is fleeting; it can be lost or destroyed. In contrast, the spiritual investments we make endure forever. When we focus on eternal treasures, we shift our perspective from the temporary to the everlasting. The most valuable assets we can make are in the lives of others. This includes mentoring, teaching, and supporting those in need, all contributing to their spiritual growth and understanding of God's love. Your financial resources can be a powerful tool in advancing the Gospel and supporting ministries that spread the message of Christ. When you invest in these endeavors, you contribute to a legacy that impacts countless lives for eternity. Your actions speak louder than words. Living a life devoted to Christ provides a living example of faith for future generations to emulate. This includes regular prayer, studying Scripture, and demonstrating love and kindness to others. Teach your children and grandchildren the values that guide your life. Emphasize the importance of integrity, compassion, generosity, and reliance on God. Share stories of how these principles have shaped your life and led to blessings. Create opportunities for your family to serve others together. Whether volunteering at a local charity or participating in church missions, these experiences deepen their understanding of God's love and the importance of giving back.

Allocate a portion of your wealth to support ministries that align with your values. This advances God's work and exemplifies the importance of prioritizing Kingdom work for your heirs. Consider creating a family foundation focused on charitable giving. This formalizes your commitment to generosity and allows future generations to carry on the mission of giving. Instill the habit of tithing within your family. Emphasizing the importance of returning a portion of one's income to God teaches future generations to trust Him and prioritize spiritual over material wealth. The spiritual impact you make will echo through generations. When you prioritize investing in what truly matters —people's lives and the Kingdom of God—you leave behind a legacy that future generations can build upon. As you model and encourage generosity, you help cultivate a family culture that values giving and service. This culture will continue to influence your descendants long after you're gone. Ultimately, investing in eternal treasures not only blesses others but also brings fulfillment and joy to your life. As you align your wealth with God's purposes, you experience the true richness of life—one filled with purpose and significance. Leaving a legacy transcending generations involves focusing on what truly matters—spiritual investments that impact lives and advance the Kingdom of God. By modeling a life of faith, instilling values, and using your wealth for God's purposes, you ensure that your legacy will last far beyond your earthly existence. As you invest in eternal treasures, you prepare future generations to continue this vital work, ensuring that the impact of your life is felt long after you are gone. In doing so, you fulfill the calling to steward the blessings God has entrusted you, creating a ripple effect that extends into eternity.

CONCLUSION

Embracing A Higher Vision For Wealth

Wealth, as presented in Scripture, is not merely a tool for personal gain or luxury; instead, it serves a much greater purpose. God has a specific plan for the resources He entrusts to us, and our responsibility is to align our financial lives with His Kingdom's principles. The foundation of our approach to wealth must always begin with Matthew 6:33, where Jesus instructs: "But seek ye first the kingdom of God, and his righteousness; and all these things shall be added unto you." When we prioritize God's Kingdom—meaning we focus on His will, righteousness, and purposes—everything else, including wealth, will naturally fall into place. Jesus reminds us that God is not against our needs being met but wants us to seek His plans for our lives first. When we trust God and focus on His mission, He provides what we need and more. Wealth should never be the ultimate goal in life. Instead, the ultimate goal is living in alignment with God's will, seeking His purposes, and obeying His Word. When we do this, financial blessings come as a byproduct, not as the primary pursuit. One of the critical lessons from Scripture is that wealth is never meant to be an end in itself. It is a tool for fulfilling God's purposes on earth. Throughout this book, we have explored the idea that financial blessings are not just for personal satisfaction or security. God blesses us so that we can be a blessing to others. Genesis 12:2 reflected this truth when God said to Abraham, "And I will make of thee a great nation, and I will bless thee, and make thy name great, and thou shalt be a blessing." Here, we see that God's blessing comes with the expectation that Abraham would, in turn, bless others.

As believers, we must adopt this mindset. Our wealth is not just for us but for advancing the Kingdom of God, helping those in need, and supporting ministries that spread the gospel. In 1 Timothy 6:17- 19, Paul encourages those who are rich not to put their trust in wealth but rather to be rich in good works, to give generously, and to store treasures in heaven. This passage teaches us that our wealth is a resource that can be used for eternal purposes. We store eternal rewards when we give generously and invest in God's Kingdom. Wealth, according to God's design, requires wise stewardship. We have learned that God is the owner of everything, and we are simply caretakers of His resources. Everything we have comes from God, and we are expected to manage it in a way that honors Him. When we are faithful to what He gives us, He can trust us even more. Stewardship also means having the right attitude toward money. Proverbs 3:9-10 *"Honour the Lord with thy substance, and with the first fruits of all thine increase: So shall thy barns be filled with plenty, and thy presses shall burst out with new wine."* We honor God with our wealth by giving back to Him. When we put God first in our finances, He blesses us abundantly. A heart of generosity is central to God's plan for wealth.

God is the ultimate giver, and as His children, we are called to reflect His character. 2 Corinthians 9:6-7 *"But this I say, He which soweth sparingly shall also reap sparingly, and he which soweth bountifully shall also reap bountifully. Every man according as he purposeth in his heart, so let him give; not grudgingly, or of necessity: for God loveth a cheerful giver."* God blesses those who give freely and cheerfully. Generosity is not just about money—it's about having a heart that is open to meeting the needs of others.

Proverbs 19:17 says: "He that hath pity upon the poor lendeth unto the Lord, and that which he hath given will he pay him again." When we give to those in need, we essentially give to God, who promises to repay us. Generosity also breaks the hold that materialism can have on our hearts. By giving, we demonstrate that our trust is in God, not in our wealth. It keeps us from becoming too attached to money and reminds us that everything we have belongs to God. Luke 6:38, *"Give, and it shall be given unto you; good measure, pressed down, shaken together, and running over, shall men give into your bosom."* When we are generous, we open the door for God's abundant blessings to flow back into our lives.

Part of God's plan for wealth is to leave a legacy that honors Him. We are not just called to accumulate wealth for ourselves but to think about how to pass on a godly inheritance to future generations. This includes not only financial wealth but also spiritual values and principles.

Leaving a legacy means teaching the next generation how to manage wealth wisely, be generous, and use their resources to advance the Kingdom of God. It is about equipping them with the understanding that wealth is a tool to serve God and bless others. By doing this, we ensure that our financial blessings continue to have an impact long after we are gone. Finally, we must always keep an eternal perspective on wealth. Jesus reminds us in Matthew 6:19-21: "Lay not up for yourselves treasures upon earth, where moth and rust doth corrupt, and where thieves break through and steal: But lay up for yourselves treasures in heaven, where neither moth nor rust doth corrupt, and where thieves do not break through nor steal: For where your treasure is, there will your heart be also." Earthly wealth is temporary, but how we use it can have eternal consequences. Wealth should never become our ultimate focus. Instead, we are to invest in what matters most to God—loving others, sharing the gospel, and making a difference in His Kingdom. These are the things that last forever.

When we focus on storing treasures in heaven, we align our hearts with God's eternal purposes. Wealth is a gift from God, meant to be used for His glory. God's plan for prosperity in the life of a believer is not about accumulating riches for selfish reasons. It's about using our resources to advance His Kingdom, bless others, and leave a lasting legacy. Colossians 3:23-24 tells us: "And whatsoever ye do, do it heartily, as to the Lord, and not unto men; Knowing that of the Lord ye shall receive the reward of the inheritance: for ye serve the Lord Christ." Whether giving, managing wealth, or using our resources, it should always be done to serve God. We are called to live with a higher vision for wealth that transcends personal ambition and taps into God's eternal purposes. By embracing this Kingdom perspective, we can experience the true blessings of wealth and make a lasting impact on the glory of God.

A SPECIAL CALL TO SALVATION & NEW BEGINNINGS FROM APOSTLE DR. DAVID PHILEMON

D ear Beloved,

God loves you deeply and has brought you to this moment for a reason. No matter your past, His love and forgiveness are available to you.

The Bible says in John 3:16, "For God so loved the world that He gave His one and only Son, that whoever believes in Him shall not perish but have eternal life." Jesus Christ came to save you, offering you a new life of purpose and peace.

If you're ready to accept Jesus as your Lord and Savior, pray this simple prayer:

The Salvation Prayer

"Heavenly Father, I come to You in the Name of Jesus. I acknowledge that I am a sinner in need of a Savior. I believe that

Jesus Christ is Your Son, that He died for my sins, and that You raised Him from the dead. I repent of my sins and turn to You with my

Whole heart. Jesus, I ask You to come into my life. Be my Lord and my Savior. I surrender my life to You. Fill me with Your Holy Spirit, guide me on the path of righteousness, and help me to follow Your script for my life. Thank you, Father, for saving me. In the name of Jesus. Amen."

Welcome to the Family of God!

If you have just prayed this prayer, Congratulations! You are now a child of God, and heaven is rejoicing. Your journey has begun, and we're here to support you as you grow in faith and discover God's unique plans for you.

Next Steps:

• Connect with a Bible-believing church.

• Read the Bible Daily: God's Word is your guide.

• Pray Regularly: Prayer is your lifeline to God.

• Share Your Faith: Don't keep the good news to yourself.

www.ingramcontent.com/pod-product-compliance
Lightning Source LLC
Chambersburg PA
CBHW071904020426
42331CB00010B/2660